THIS BOOK BELONGS TO

_____

START DATE

_____

📖 SHE READS TRUTH

EXECUTIVE

FOUNDER/CHIEF EXECUTIVE OFFICER
Raechel Myers

CO-FOUNDER/CHIEF CONTENT OFFICER
Amanda Bible Williams

CHIEF OPERATING OFFICER
Ryan Myers

EDITORIAL

EDITORIAL DIRECTOR
Jessica Lamb

MANAGING EDITOR
Beth Joseph, MDiv

DIGITAL MANAGING EDITOR
Oghosa Iyamu, MDiv

ASSOCIATE EDITORS
Lindsey Jacobi, MDiv
Tameshia Williams, ThM

PRODUCTION EDITOR
Hannah Little, MTS

CREATIVE

CREATIVE DIRECTOR
Amy Dennis

DESIGN MANAGER
Kelsea Allen

ART DIRECTOR
Aimee Lindamood

DESIGNERS
Abbey Benson
Amanda Brush, MA
Annie Glover
Lauren Haag

JUNIOR DESIGNER
Jessie Gerakinis

MARKETING

MARKETING DIRECTOR
Kamron Kunce

SOCIAL MEDIA STRATEGIST
Taylor Krupp

OPERATIONS

OPERATIONS DIRECTOR
Allison Sutton

OFFICE MANAGER
Nicole Quirion

PROJECT ASSISTANT
Mary Beth Montgomery

SHIPPING

SHIPPING MANAGER
Marian Byne

FULFILLMENT LEAD
Cait Baggerman

FULFILLMENT SPECIALISTS
Kajsa Matheny
Noe Sanchez

SUBSCRIPTION INQUIRIES
orders@shereadstruth.com

COMMUNITY SUPPORT

COMMUNITY SUPPORT MANAGER
Kara Hewett, MOL

COMMUNITY SUPPORT SPECIALISTS
Katy McKnight
Heather Vollono
Margot Williams

CONTRIBUTOR

PHOTOGRAPHY
Madeline Mullenbach (47, 79, 151, 183)

@SHEREADSTRUTH

Download the
She Reads Truth app,
available for iOS
and Android

Subscribe to the
She Reads Truth podcast

SHEREADSTRUTH.COM

SHE READS TRUTH™

© 2022 by She Reads Truth, LLC

All rights reserved.

All photography used by permission.

ISBN 978-1-952670-69-5

1 2 3 4 5 6 7 8 9 10

All Scripture is taken from the Christian Standard Bible®. Copyright © 2020 by Holman Bible Publishers. Used by permission. Christian Standard Bible® and CSB® are federally registered trademarks of Holman Bible Publishers.

Verses omitted in the CSB are also omitted in this book.

Research support provided by Logos Bible Software™. Learn more at logos.com.

This book was printed offset in Nashville, Tennessee, on 70# Lynx Opaque. Cover is Neenah Royal Sundance Linen 80#C Brilliant White.

THE LIFE OF JESUS

AS RECORDED BY MATTHEW, MARK, AND LUKE

We will look to
Scripture to learn
about Jesus and from
Jesus, inviting His life
to shape our own.

Amanda

Amanda Bible Williams
CO-FOUNDER & CHIEF
CONTENT OFFICER

In the Williams house, music matters. There's a song for every occasion, a lyric for every emotion, and a soundtrack for every season. We listen to a wide range of music and in a variety of ways—in the car with the windows rolled down, on a vinyl record player in the living room, even via cassette tape Walkman (yes, really). But as any music lover will testify, nothing beats experiencing the songs you love performed live by the artists who create them.

So naturally, when my twin sons saw their all-time favorite band in concert for the first time a few weeks ago, it was a very big deal. The date held its place on the family calendar for a full year. When it finally arrived, dinner plans were made, band t-shirts were donned, the merch booth was visited on the way into (and out of) the arena. And for three hours on a school night, two kids had the joy of being swept up into a new experience of the songs they knew by heart.

Dimension and perspective can bring new depth and richness to what we already know. That's what this reading plan did for me. It helped me to see anew the unchanging beauty and glory of Jesus.

For the first time as a She Reads Truth community, we will spend a full study focusing our reading on three of the four Gospels in Scripture: Matthew, Mark, and Luke. Collectively known as the Synoptic Gospels, these three books of the Bible were written by three different people, from three unique perspectives, to record the life of Jesus on earth. (If *synoptic* is a new term for you, don't worry; we'll get to that on page 17.)

By synthesizing these three narratives, we'll read about the different movements of Jesus's life and ministry, learning not just from what He taught, but how He lived. We'll see how Jesus—fully God and fully human—lived, how He responded to the people around Him, and how He interacted with God the Father. Together, we will look to Scripture to learn about Jesus and from Jesus, inviting His life to shape our own.

As I imagine this Study Book open in your hands, I'm reminded of what our teammate Hannah said in the early stages of developing this reading plan. "I found myself getting lost in the story," she marveled, and we all nodded our heads in agreement. The true story of the life and person of Jesus captivated us anew, and we pray it captivates you too.

ABCDEFGHIJK
LMNOPQRST
UVWXYZ

1234567890

Glory to God in the highest heaven, and peace on earth to people he favors. Luke 2:14

At She Reads Truth, we believe in pairing the inherently beautiful Word of God with the aesthetic beauty it deserves. Each of our resources is thoughtfully and artfully designed to highlight the beauty, goodness, and truth of Scripture in a way that reflects the themes of each curated reading plan.

The design of this Study Book is inspired by a travel journal. Simple elements like collages, photographs, and lettering throughout are meant to reflect the experience of reminiscing about a journey.

Each week of the reading plan features a unique color to represent that distinct part of Jesus's life and ministry.

HOW TO USE THIS BOOK

She Reads Truth is a community of women dedicated to reading the Word of God every day. In **The Life of Jesus** reading plan, we will read the account of Jesus Christ's life and ministry as told by Matthew, Mark, and Luke to understand the broader story of Jesus's time on earth.

READ & REFLECT

The Life of Jesus Study Book focuses primarily on Scripture, with added features to come alongside your time with God's Word.

SCRIPTURE READING

Designed for a Monday start, this Study Book presents daily readings on the major movements in Jesus's life on earth as told by Matthew, Mark, and Luke.

REFLECTION QUESTIONS

Each weekday features questions and space for personal reflection.

COMMUNITY & CONVERSATION

You can start reading this book at any time! If you want to join women from Nashville to Nigeria as they read along with you, the She Reads Truth community will start Day 1 of **The Life of Jesus** on Monday, January 2, 2023.

 SHE READS TRUTH APP

Devotionals corresponding to each daily reading can be found in **The Life of Jesus** reading plan on the She Reads Truth app. New devotionals will be published each weekday once the plan begins on Monday, January 2, 2023. You can use the app to participate in community discussion and more.

GRACE DAY

Use Saturdays to catch up on your reading, pray, and rest in the presence of the Lord.

WEEKLY TRUTH

Sundays are set aside for Scripture memorization.

See tips for memorizing Scripture on page 188.

EXTRAS

This book features additional tools to help you gain a deeper understanding of the text.

Find a complete list of extras on pages 11–13.

 SHEREADSTRUTH.COM

The Life of Jesus reading plan and devotionals will also be available at SheReadsTruth.com as the community reads each day. Invite your family, friends, and neighbors to read along with you!

 SHE READS TRUTH PODCAST

Subscribe to the She Reads Truth podcast and join our founders and their guests each week as they talk about what you'll read in the week ahead.

 *Podcast episodes 161–165 for **The Life of Jesus** series release on Mondays beginning January 2, 2023.*

Table of Contents

Jesus's Birth and Preparation for Ministry

Jesus Ministers in Galilee

Jesus and His Public Ministry

Key Passage

Jesus continued going around to all the towns and villages, teaching in their synagogues, preaching the good news of the kingdom, and healing every disease and every sickness. When he saw the crowds, he felt compassion for them, because they were distressed and dejected, like sheep without a shepherd.

——

MATTHEW 9:35–36

Introduction

—

Who is Jesus Christ? The New Testament books of Matthew, Mark, and Luke answer this question in their narrative accounts. Over five weeks, this reading plan connects passages from these three Gospels to tell the story of Jesus's life on earth.

The Synoptic Gospels

Matthew, Mark, and Luke are known as the "Synoptic Gospels." The title comes from the Greek word *synopsis*, meaning "viewed together," because the three books record events from the life of Jesus from a similar perspective.

All three of these books...

1. *Cover much of the same material.*
2. *Follow the same general outline.*
3. *Emphasize the first part of Jesus's ministry in Galilee.*
4. *Record Jesus's teachings in parables and short sayings.*
5. *Focus on the kingdom of God and the power of Jesus.*

Who Were Matthew, Mark, and Luke?

Most Bible scholars are convinced Mark was the earliest Gospel written and that it served as one of the sources for the writing of Matthew and Luke.

Though the Gospel of Mark is anonymous, the author is believed to be John Mark. He was the son of a Jewish widow named Mary, in whose house the church in Jerusalem sometimes gathered (Ac 12:12–17) and where Jesus possibly ate the Last Supper with His disciples. Mark relied on the eyewitness testimony of Peter, one of Jesus's disciples, as the source for his account.

Though he did not identify himself in the text, the early Church unanimously affirmed that the apostle Matthew authored the Gospel of Matthew. Also known as Levi, Matthew was called to follow Jesus while he was working as a tax collector (Mt 9:9). The Gospel of Luke was written by a physician and non-Jewish convert to Christianity, Luke, who traveled with Paul on his missionary journeys.

WHAT ABOUT THE GOSPEL OF JOHN?

The content, themes, and order of events in John are distinct, with a special emphasis on festival dates, theological implications, and preparing Jesus's disciples. While no less important or powerful, John's unique flow and content set it apart from the Synoptic Gospels.

Why Are There Four Gospels?

—

The four Gospels in Scripture are books dedicated to telling the story of the life, death, and resurrection of Jesus Christ. Since the early days of Christianity, the Church has recognized four Gospels as giving reliable accounts of the story of Christ: Matthew, Mark, Luke, and John. But why does the Bible include four separate accounts?

Each Gospel verifies the authenticity of the others. The four writers had a strong connection to Jesus, either as an apostle or as someone close with an apostle. The varied accounts help us see Jesus from different perspectives—providing more dimension to the picture than we would get from only one account—while also remaining true to the central message that unites them.

Gospel	Original Audience	Presents Jesus As	Some Unique Features
Matthew	Jews	The fulfillment of Old Testament promises **MT 1:1, 22–23; 2:15; 4:14–16; 5:17; 21:9; 26:56**	Longer recording of the Beatitudes The five discourses Many parables
Mark	Romans	Suffering Son of Man **MK 8:31; 9:12; 10:45**	Fast-paced and action-oriented Focused more on the narrative Most concise Gospel
Luke	Most honorable Theophilus Gentiles	The awaited Messiah **LK 1:51–55; 2:11; 9:18–20**	Lengthy nativity story Focused on historical detail Includes extended narratives Emphasis on ministry to the marginalized More parables than any other Gospel
John	Everyone	The divine Son of God **JN 1:14, 34; 20:31**	Poetic voice "I Am" statements Focused on the week before Jesus's death

Tips for Reading the Synoptic Gospels

Remember that these books are historical literature.

Matthew, Mark, and Luke record events that took place in real time and history and were written to present accurate historical information.

Remember that the Synoptic Gospels are theological literature.

A *Gospel* in Scripture is a book dedicated to telling the story of the life, death, and resurrection of Jesus Christ. The *gospel*, or "good news," is what Jesus Christ has done to restore broken creation and sinful people to their holy Creator. The purpose of the Synoptic Gospels is not only to record history but also to encourage believers and convince nonbelievers of the truth of the good news of Jesus.

Remember that each one is a narrative.

While documenting true events, each Gospel is also a unique literary work. Each author emphasized different details on the same historical events about Jesus's ministry on earth.

Remember that the Synoptic Gospels tell one story.

While each account highlights something different, together they give a more complete look at Jesus's life and ministry. As you read, notice who Jesus is, how people interacted with Him, and how we can respond to Him.

Gabriel Predicts Jesus's Birth

———

Therefore, the holy one to be born will be called the Son of God.

LUKE 1:35

WEEK 01   DAY 01

Luke 1:1–38

The Dedication to Theophilus

Many have undertaken to compile a narrative about the events that have been fulfilled among us, [2] just as the original eyewitnesses and servants of the word handed them down to us. [3] So it also seemed good to me, since I have carefully investigated everything from the very first, to write to you in an orderly sequence, most honorable Theophilus, [4] so that you may know the certainty of the things about which you have been instructed.

Gabriel Predicts John's Birth

[5] In the days of King Herod of Judea, there was a priest of Abijah's division named Zechariah. His wife was from the daughters of Aaron, and her name was Elizabeth. [6] Both were righteous in God's sight, living without blame according to all the commands and requirements of the Lord. [7] But they had no children because Elizabeth could not conceive, and both of them were well along in years.

[8] When his division was on duty and he was serving as priest before God, [9] it happened that he was chosen by lot, according to the custom of the priesthood, to enter the sanctuary of the Lord and burn incense. [10] At the hour of incense the whole assembly of the people was praying outside. [11] An angel of the Lord appeared to him, standing to the right of the altar of incense. [12] When Zechariah saw him, he was terrified and overcome with fear. [13] But the angel said to him, "Do not be afraid, Zechariah, because your prayer has been heard. Your wife Elizabeth will bear you a son, and you will name him John. [14] There will be joy and delight for you, and many will rejoice at his birth. [15] For he will be great in the sight of the Lord and will never drink wine or beer. He will be filled with the Holy Spirit while still in his mother's womb. [16] He will turn many of the children of Israel to the Lord their God. [17] And he will go before him in the spirit and power of Elijah, to turn the hearts of fathers to their children, and the disobedient to the understanding of the righteous, to make ready for the Lord a prepared people."

[18] "How can I know this?" Zechariah asked the angel. "For I am an old man, and my wife is well along in years."

19 The angel answered him, "I am Gabriel, who stands in the presence of God, and I was sent to speak to you and tell you this good news. 20 Now listen. You will become silent and unable to speak until the day these things take place, because you did not believe my words, which will be fulfilled in their proper time."

21 Meanwhile, the people were waiting for Zechariah, amazed that he stayed so long in the sanctuary. 22 When he did come out, he could not speak to them. Then they realized that he had seen a vision in the sanctuary. He was making signs to them and remained speechless. 23 When the days of his ministry were completed, he went back home.

24 After these days his wife Elizabeth conceived and kept herself in seclusion for five months. She said, 25 "The Lord has done this for me. He has looked with favor in these days to take away my disgrace among the people."

Gabriel Predicts Jesus's Birth

26 In the sixth month, the angel Gabriel was sent by God to a town in Galilee called Nazareth, 27 to a virgin engaged to a man named Joseph, of the house of David. The virgin's name was Mary. 28 And the angel came to her and said, "Greetings, favored woman! The Lord is with you." 29 But she was deeply troubled by this statement, wondering what kind of greeting this could be. 30 Then the angel told her, "Do not be afraid, Mary, for you have found favor with God. 31 Now listen: You will conceive and give birth to a son, and you will name him Jesus.

32 He will be great and will be called the Son of the Most High,

and the Lord God will give him the throne of his father David. 33 He will reign over the house of Jacob forever, and his kingdom will have no end."

34 Mary asked the angel, "How can this be, since I have not had sexual relations with a man?"

35 The angel replied to her, "The Holy Spirit will come upon you, and the power of the Most High will overshadow you. Therefore, the holy one to be born will be called the Son of God. 36 And consider your relative Elizabeth—even she has conceived a son in her old age, and this is the sixth month for her who was called childless. 37 For nothing will be impossible with God."

38 "See, I am the Lord's servant," said Mary. "May it happen to me as you have said." Then the angel left her.

SUMMARIZE TODAY'S READING.

The Synoptic Gospels, written in narrative form, invite us into the story of Jesus's life on earth.
Use this space every day to sum up the narrative in your own words.

WHAT IS SOMETHING I LEARNED OR WAS REMINDED OF ABOUT JESUS?

Use this question as a prompt to reflect on the character and nature of Jesus as you read.

WHAT DID I NOTICE ABOUT HOW THE PEOPLE IN TODAY'S STORY PREPARED FOR JESUS'S ARRIVAL?

In Jesus, God walked on earth, miraculously entering into the lives of real first-century men and women.
Use this question to reflect on how they reacted to the news of the coming child.

Praise for the Savior and Messiah

He has raised up a horn of salvation for us in the house of his servant David.

LUKE 1:69

Luke 1:39–80

Mary's Visit to Elizabeth

³⁹ In those days Mary set out and hurried to a town in the hill country of Judah ⁴⁰ where she entered Zechariah's house and greeted Elizabeth. ⁴¹ When Elizabeth heard Mary's greeting, the baby leaped inside her, and Elizabeth was filled with the Holy Spirit. ⁴² Then she exclaimed with a loud cry, "Blessed are you among women, and your child will be blessed! ⁴³ How could this happen to me, that the mother of my Lord should come to me? ⁴⁴ For you see, when the sound of your greeting reached my ears, the baby leaped for joy inside me. ⁴⁵ Blessed is she who has believed that the Lord would fulfill what he has spoken to her!"

Mary's Praise

⁴⁶ And Mary said:

> My soul magnifies the Lord,
> ⁴⁷ and my spirit rejoices in God my Savior,
> ⁴⁸ because he has looked with favor
> on the humble condition of his servant.
> Surely, from now on all generations
> will call me blessed,
> ⁴⁹ because the Mighty One
> has done great things for me,
> and his name is holy.
> ⁵⁰ His mercy is from generation to generation
> on those who fear him.
> ⁵¹ He has done a mighty deed with his arm;
> he has scattered the proud
> because of the thoughts of their hearts;
> ⁵² he has toppled the mighty from their thrones
> and exalted the lowly.
> ⁵³ He has satisfied the hungry with good things
> and sent the rich away empty.
> ⁵⁴ He has helped his servant Israel,
> remembering his mercy
> ⁵⁵ to Abraham and his descendants forever,
> just as he spoke to our ancestors.

⁵⁶ And Mary stayed with her about three months; then she returned to her home.

The Birth and Naming of John

⁵⁷ Now the time had come for Elizabeth to give birth, and she had a son. ⁵⁸ Then her neighbors and relatives heard that the Lord had shown her his great mercy, and they rejoiced with her.

⁵⁹ When they came to circumcise the child on the eighth day, they were going to name him Zechariah, after his father. ⁶⁰ But his mother responded, "No. He will be called John."

⁶¹ Then they said to her, "None of your relatives has that name." ⁶² So they motioned to his father to find out what he wanted him to be called. ⁶³ He asked for a writing tablet and wrote, "His name is John." And they were all amazed. ⁶⁴ Immediately his mouth was opened and his tongue set free, and he began to speak, praising God. ⁶⁵ Fear came on all those who lived around them, and all these things were being talked about throughout the hill country of Judea. ⁶⁶ All who heard about him took it to heart, saying, "What then will this child become?" For, indeed, the Lord's hand was with him.

Zechariah's Prophecy

⁶⁷ Then his father Zechariah was filled with the Holy Spirit and prophesied:

⁶⁸ Blessed is the Lord, the God of Israel,
because he has visited
and provided redemption for his people.
⁶⁹ He has raised up a horn of salvation for us
in the house of his servant David,
⁷⁰ just as he spoke by the mouth
of his holy prophets in ancient times;
⁷¹ salvation from our enemies
and from the hand of those who hate us.
⁷² He has dealt mercifully with our ancestors
and remembered his holy covenant—
⁷³ the oath that he swore to our father Abraham,
to grant that we,
⁷⁴ having been rescued
from the hand of our enemies,
would serve him without fear

⁷⁵ in holiness and righteousness
in his presence all our days.
⁷⁶ And you, child, will be called
a prophet of the Most High,
for you will go before the Lord
to prepare his ways,
⁷⁷ to give his people knowledge of salvation
through the forgiveness of their sins.
⁷⁸ Because of our God's merciful compassion,
the dawn from on high will visit us
⁷⁹ to shine on those who live in darkness
and the shadow of death,
to guide our feet into the way of peace.

⁸⁰ The child grew up and became strong in spirit, and he was in the wilderness until the day of his public appearance to Israel.

Matthew 1:18–25

The Nativity of the Messiah

¹⁸ The birth of Jesus Christ came about this way: After his mother Mary had been engaged to Joseph, it was discovered before they came together that she was pregnant from the Holy Spirit. ¹⁹ So her husband, Joseph, being a righteous man, and not wanting to disgrace her publicly, decided to divorce her secretly.

²⁰ But after he had considered these things, an angel of the Lord appeared to him in a dream, saying, "Joseph, son of David, don't be afraid to take Mary as your wife, because what has been conceived in her is from the Holy Spirit. ²¹ She will give birth to a son, and you are to name him Jesus, because he will save his people from their sins."

²² Now all this took place to fulfill what was spoken by the Lord through the prophet:

> ²³ See, the virgin will become pregnant
> and give birth to a son,
> and they will name him Immanuel,

which is translated "God is with us."

[24] When Joseph woke up, he did as the Lord's angel had commanded him. He married her [25] but did not have sexual relations with her until she gave birth to a son. And he named him Jesus.

Luke 2:1–38

The Birth of Jesus

[1] In those days a decree went out from Caesar Augustus that the whole empire should be registered. [2] This first registration took place while Quirinius was governing Syria. [3] So everyone went to be registered, each to his own town.

[4] Joseph also went up from the town of Nazareth in Galilee, to Judea, to the city of David, which is called Bethlehem, because he was of the house and family line of David, [5] to be registered along with Mary, who was engaged to him and was pregnant. [6] While they were there, the time came for her to give birth. [7] Then she gave birth to her firstborn son, and she wrapped him tightly in cloth and laid him in a manger, because there was no guest room available for them.

The Shepherds and the Angels

[8] In the same region, shepherds were staying out in the fields and keeping watch at night over their flock. [9] Then an angel of the Lord stood before them, and the glory of the Lord shone around them, and they were terrified. [10] But the angel said to them, "Don't be afraid, for look,

I proclaim to you good news of great joy that will be for all the people:

[11] Today in the city of David a Savior was born for you, who is the Messiah, the Lord. [12] This will be the sign for you: You will find a baby wrapped tightly in cloth and lying in a manger."

[13] Suddenly there was a multitude of the heavenly host with the angel, praising God and saying:

¹⁴ Glory to God in the highest heaven,
and peace on earth to people he favors!

¹⁵ When the angels had left them and returned to heaven, the shepherds said to one another, "Let's go straight to Bethlehem and see what has happened, which the Lord has made known to us."

¹⁶ They hurried off and found both Mary and Joseph, and the baby who was lying in the manger. ¹⁷ After seeing them, they reported the message they were told about this child, ¹⁸ and all who heard it were amazed at what the shepherds said to them. ¹⁹ But Mary was treasuring up all these things in her heart and meditating on them. ²⁰ The shepherds returned, glorifying and praising God for all the things they had seen and heard, which were just as they had been told.

The Circumcision and Presentation of Jesus

²¹ When the eight days were completed for his circumcision, he was named Jesus—the name given by the angel before he was conceived. ²² And when the days of their purification according to the law of Moses were finished, they brought him up to Jerusalem to present him to the Lord ²³ (just as it is written in the law of the Lord, Every firstborn male will be dedicated to the Lord) ²⁴ and to offer a sacrifice (according to what is stated in the law of the Lord, a pair of turtledoves or two young pigeons).

Simeon's Prophetic Praise

²⁵ There was a man in Jerusalem whose name was Simeon. This man was righteous and devout, looking forward to Israel's consolation, and the Holy Spirit was on him. ²⁶ It had been revealed to him by the Holy Spirit that he would not see death before he saw the Lord's Messiah. ²⁷ Guided by the Spirit, he entered the temple. When the parents brought in the child Jesus to perform for him what was customary under the law, ²⁸ Simeon took him up in his arms, praised God, and said,

²⁹ Now, Master,

you can dismiss your servant in peace,

as you promised.

³⁰ For my eyes have seen your salvation.

³¹ You have prepared it

in the presence of all peoples—

³² a light for revelation to the Gentiles

and glory to your people Israel.

³³ His father and mother were amazed at what was being said about him. ³⁴ Then Simeon blessed them and told his mother Mary, "Indeed, this child is destined to cause the fall and rise of many in Israel and to be a sign that will be opposed— ³⁵ and a sword will pierce your own soul—that the thoughts of many hearts may be revealed."

Anna's Testimony

³⁶ There was also a prophetess, Anna, a daughter of Phanuel, of the tribe of Asher. She was well along in years, having lived with her husband seven years after her marriage, ³⁷ and was a widow for eighty-four years. She did not leave the temple, serving God night and day with fasting and prayers. ³⁸ At that very moment, she came up and began to thank God and to speak about him to all who were looking forward to the redemption of Jerusalem.

DATE   /   /

SUMMARIZE TODAY'S READING.

WHAT IS SOMETHING I LEARNED OR WAS REMINDED OF ABOUT JESUS?

WHAT DID I NOTICE ABOUT THE WAY JESUS LIVED HIS LIFE?

Jesus taught not only in parables and sermons, but in how He lived and served on earth.
Use this question to reflect on what Jesus's fully human habits and practices model for life today.

In His Father's House

Jesus increased in wisdom and stature, and in favor with God and with people.

LUKE 2:52

WEEK 01   DAY 04

Matthew 2

Wise Men Visit the King

After Jesus was born in Bethlehem of Judea in the days of King Herod, wise men from the east arrived in Jerusalem, ² saying, "Where is he who has been born king of the Jews? For we saw his star at its rising and have come to worship him."

³ When King Herod heard this, he was deeply disturbed, and all Jerusalem with him. ⁴ So he assembled all the chief priests and scribes of the people and asked them where the Messiah would be born.

⁵ "In Bethlehem of Judea," they told him, "because this is what was written by the prophet:

⁶ And you, Bethlehem, in the land of Judah,
are by no means least among the rulers of Judah:

Because out of you will come a ruler
who will shepherd my people Israel."

⁷ Then Herod secretly summoned the wise men and asked them the exact time the star appeared. ⁸ He sent them to Bethlehem and said, "Go and search carefully for the child. When you find him, report back to me so that I too can go and worship him."

⁹ After hearing the king, they went on their way. And there it was—the star they had seen at its rising. It led them until it came and stopped above the place where the child was. ¹⁰ When they saw the star, they were overwhelmed with joy. ¹¹ Entering the house, they saw the child with Mary his mother, and falling to their knees, they worshiped him. Then they opened their treasures and presented him with gifts:

gold, frankincense, and myrrh. ¹² And being warned in a dream not to go back to Herod, they returned to their own country by another route.

The Flight into Egypt

¹³ After they were gone, an angel of the Lord appeared to Joseph in a dream, saying, "Get up! Take the child and his mother, flee to Egypt, and stay there until I tell you. For Herod is about to search for the child to kill him." ¹⁴ So he got up, took the child and his mother during the night, and escaped to Egypt. ¹⁵ He stayed there until Herod's death, so that what was spoken by the Lord through the prophet might be fulfilled: Out of Egypt I called my Son.

The Massacre of the Innocents

¹⁶ Then Herod, when he realized that he had been outwitted by the wise men, flew into a rage. He gave orders to massacre all the boys in and around Bethlehem who were two years old and under, in keeping with the time he had learned from the wise men. ¹⁷ Then what was spoken through Jeremiah the prophet was fulfilled:

¹⁸ A voice was heard in Ramah,

weeping, and great mourning,
Rachel weeping for her children;
and she refused to be consoled,
because they are no more.

The Return to Nazareth

¹⁹ After Herod died, an angel of the Lord appeared in a dream to Joseph in Egypt, ²⁰ saying, "Get up, take the child and his mother, and go to the land of Israel, because those who intended to kill the child are dead." ²¹ So he got up, took the child and his mother, and entered the land of Israel. ²² But when he heard that Archelaus was ruling over Judea in place of his father Herod, he was afraid to go there. And being warned in a dream, he withdrew to the region of Galilee. ²³ Then he went and settled in a town called Nazareth to fulfill what was spoken through the prophets, that he would be called a Nazarene.

Luke 2:39–52

The Family's Return to Nazareth

³⁹ When they had completed everything according to the law of the Lord, they returned to Galilee, to their own town of Nazareth. ⁴⁰ The boy grew up and became strong, filled with wisdom, and God's grace was on him.

In His Father's House

41 Every year his parents traveled to Jerusalem for the Passover Festival. 42 When he was twelve years old, they went up according to the custom of the festival. 43 After those days were over, as they were returning, the boy Jesus stayed behind in Jerusalem, but his parents did not know it. 44 Assuming he was in the traveling party, they went a day's journey. Then they began looking for him among their relatives and friends. 45 When they did not find him, they returned to Jerusalem to search for him. 46 After three days, they found him in the temple sitting among the teachers, listening to them and asking them questions. 47 And all those who heard him were astounded at his understanding and his answers. 48 When his parents saw him, they were astonished, and his mother said to him, "Son, why have you treated us like this? Your father and I have been anxiously searching for you."

49 "Why were you searching for me?" he asked them. "Didn't you know that it was necessary for me to be in my Father's house?" 50 But they did not understand what he said to them.

In Favor with God and with People

51 Then he went down with them and came to Nazareth and was obedient to them. His mother kept all these things in her heart. 52 And Jesus increased in wisdom and stature, and in favor with God and with people.

DATE   /   /

SUMMARIZE TODAY'S READING.

WHAT IS SOMETHING I LEARNED OR WAS REMINDED OF ABOUT JESUS?

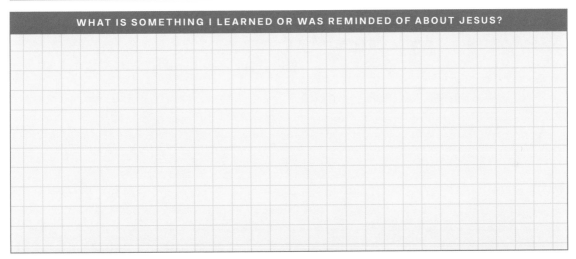

WHAT DID I NOTICE ABOUT THE WAY JESUS LIVED HIS LIFE?

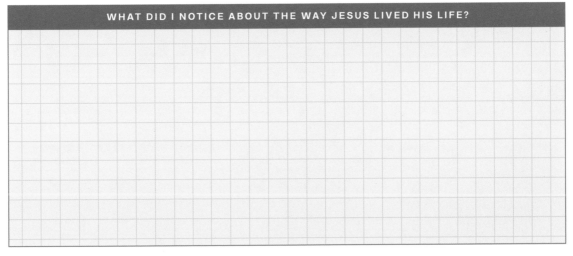

The Temptation of Jesus

"Man must not live on bread alone."

LUKE 4:4

Luke 3:1–22

The Messiah's Herald

In the fifteenth year of the reign of Tiberius Caesar, while Pontius Pilate was governor of Judea, Herod was tetrarch of Galilee, his brother Philip tetrarch of the region of Iturea and Trachonitis, and Lysanias tetrarch of Abilene, ² during the high priesthood of Annas and Caiaphas, God's word came to John the son of Zechariah in the wilderness. ³ He went into all the vicinity of the Jordan, proclaiming a baptism of repentance for the forgiveness of sins, ⁴ as it is written in the book of the words of the prophet Isaiah:

A voice of one crying out in the wilderness:
Prepare the way for the Lord;
make his paths straight!
⁵ Every valley will be filled,
and every mountain and hill will be made low;
the crooked will become straight,
the rough ways smooth,
⁶ and everyone will see the salvation of God.

⁷ He then said to the crowds who came out to be baptized by him, "Brood of vipers! Who warned you to flee from the coming wrath? ⁸ Therefore produce fruit consistent with repentance. And don't start saying to yourselves, 'We have Abraham as our father,' for I tell you that God is able to raise up children for Abraham from these stones. ⁹ The ax is already at the root of the trees. Therefore, every tree that doesn't produce good fruit will be cut down and thrown into the fire."

¹⁰ "What then should we do?" the crowds were asking him.

[11] He replied to them, "The one who has two shirts must share with someone who has none, and the one who has food must do the same."

[12] Tax collectors also came to be baptized, and they asked him, "Teacher, what should we do?"

[13] He told them, "Don't collect any more than what you have been authorized."

[14] Some soldiers also questioned him, "What should we do?"

He said to them, "Don't take money from anyone by force or false accusation, and be satisfied with your wages."

[15] Now the people were waiting expectantly, and all of them were questioning in their hearts whether John might be the Messiah. [16] John answered them all, "I baptize you with water, but one who is more powerful than I am is coming. I am not worthy to untie the strap of his sandals. He will baptize you with the Holy Spirit and fire. [17] His winnowing shovel is in his hand to clear his threshing floor and gather the wheat into his barn, but the chaff he will burn with fire that never goes out." [18] Then, along with many other exhortations, he proclaimed good news to the people. [19] But when John rebuked Herod the tetrarch because of Herodias, his brother's wife, and all the evil things he had done, [20] Herod added this to everything else—he locked up John in prison.

The Baptism of Jesus

[21] When all the people were baptized, Jesus also was baptized. As he was praying, heaven opened, [22] and the Holy Spirit descended on him in a physical appearance like a dove. And a voice came from heaven:

"You are my beloved Son; with you I am well-pleased."

Mark 1:1–8

The Messiah's Herald

[1] The beginning of the gospel of Jesus Christ, the Son of God. [2] As it is written in Isaiah the prophet:

See, I am sending my messenger ahead of you;
he will prepare your way.
³ A voice of one crying out in the wilderness:
Prepare the way for the Lord;
make his paths straight!

⁴ John came baptizing in the wilderness and proclaiming a baptism of repentance for the forgiveness of sins. ⁵ The whole Judean countryside and all the people of Jerusalem were going out to him, and they were baptized by him in the Jordan River, confessing their sins. ⁶ John wore a camel-hair garment with a leather belt around his waist and ate locusts and wild honey.

⁷ He proclaimed, "One who is more powerful than I am is coming after me. I am not worthy to stoop down and untie the strap of his sandals. ⁸ I baptize you with water, but he will baptize you with the Holy Spirit."

Matthew 3:13–16

The Baptism of Jesus

¹³ Then Jesus came from Galilee to John at the Jordan, to be baptized by him. ¹⁴ But John tried to stop him, saying, "I need to be baptized by you, and yet you come to me?"

¹⁵ Jesus answered him, "Allow it for now, because this is the way for us to fulfill all righteousness." Then John allowed him to be baptized.

¹⁶ When Jesus was baptized, he went up immediately from the water. The heavens suddenly opened for him, and he saw the Spirit of God descending like a dove and coming down on him.

Luke 4:1–13

The Temptation of Jesus

¹ Then Jesus left the Jordan, full of the Holy Spirit, and was led by the Spirit in the wilderness ² for forty days to be tempted by the devil. He ate nothing during those days, and when they were over, he was hungry. ³ The devil said to him, "If you are the Son of God, tell this stone to become bread."

THESE MARGIN NOTES INDICATE WHERE YOU CAN FIND A PARALLEL ACCOUNT IN THE OTHER SYNOPTIC GOSPELS.

SEE MT 4:1–11

[4] But Jesus answered him, "It is written: Man must not live on bread alone."

[5] So he took him up and showed him all the kingdoms of the world in a moment of time. [6] The devil said to him, "I will give you their splendor and all this authority, because it has been given over to me, and I can give it to anyone I want. [7] If you, then, will worship me, all will be yours."

[8] And Jesus answered him, "It is written:

Worship the Lord your God, and serve him only."

[9] So he took him to Jerusalem, had him stand on the pinnacle of the temple, and said to him, "If you are the Son of God, throw yourself down from here. [10] For it is written:

He will give his angels orders concerning you,
to protect you, [11] and
they will support you with their hands,
so that you will not strike
your foot against a stone."

[12] And Jesus answered him, "It is said: Do not test the Lord your God."

[13] After the devil had finished every temptation, he departed from him for a time.

DATE   /   /

SUMMARIZE TODAY'S READING.

WHAT IS SOMETHING I LEARNED OR WAS REMINDED OF ABOUT JESUS?

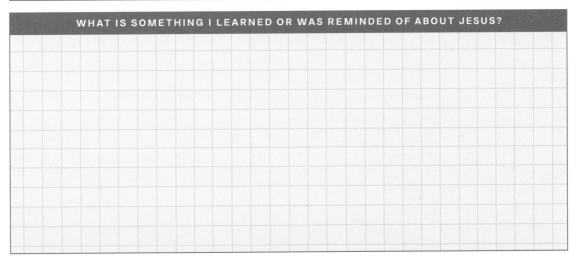

WHAT DID I NOTICE ABOUT THE WAY JESUS LIVED HIS LIFE?

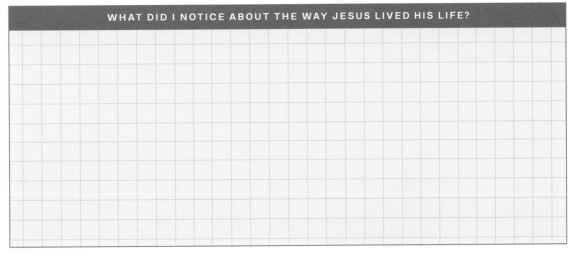

Grace Day

Take this day to catch up on your reading, pray, and rest in the presence of the Lord.

Glory to God in the highest heaven, and peace on earth to people he favors!

Luke 2:14

Weekly Truth

Scripture is God-breathed and true. When we memorize it, we carry the good news of Jesus with us wherever we go.

For this study, we will memorize our key passage, Matthew 9:35–36. This week we will start with the first part of verse 35, which begins to describe Jesus's ministry.

Jesus continued going around to all the towns and villages, teaching in their synagogues, preaching the good news of the kingdom, and healing every disease and every sickness. When he saw the crowds, he felt compassion for them, because they were distressed and dejected, like sheep without a shepherd.

MATTHEW 9:35–36

See tips for memorizing Scripture on page 188.

Jesus Forgives and Heals

"The Son of Man has authority on earth to forgive sins."

MARK 2:10

Matthew 4:12–17

Ministry in Galilee

12 When he heard that John had been arrested, he withdrew into Galilee. 13 He left Nazareth and went to live in Capernaum by the sea, in the region of Zebulun and Naphtali. 14 This was to fulfill what was spoken through the prophet Isaiah:

15 Land of Zebulun and land of Naphtali,
along the road by the sea, beyond the Jordan,
Galilee of the Gentiles.
16 The people who live in darkness
have seen a great light,
and for those living in the land of the shadow of death,
a light has dawned.

17 From then on Jesus began to preach, "Repent, because the kingdom of heaven has come near."

Mark 1:14–45

Ministry in Galilee

14 After John was arrested, Jesus went to Galilee, proclaiming the good news of God: 15 "The time is fulfilled, and the kingdom of God has come near. Repent and believe the good news!"

The First Disciples

16 As he passed alongside the Sea of Galilee, he saw Simon and Andrew, Simon's brother, casting a net into the sea—for they were fishermen. 17 "Follow me," Jesus told them, "and I will make you fish for people." 18 Immediately they left their nets and followed him. 19 Going on a little farther, he saw James the son of Zebedee and his brother John in a boat putting their nets in order. 20 Immediately he called them, and they left their father Zebedee in the boat with the hired men and followed him.

SEE MT 4:18–22

Driving Out an Unclean Spirit

SEE LK 4:31–37

[21] They went into Capernaum, and right away he entered the synagogue on the Sabbath and began to teach. [22] They were astonished at his teaching because he was teaching them as one who had authority, and not like the scribes.

[23] Just then a man with an unclean spirit was in their synagogue. He cried out, [24] "What do you have to do with us, Jesus of Nazareth? Have you come to destroy us? I know who you are—the Holy One of God!"

[25] Jesus rebuked him saying, "Be silent, and come out of him!" [26] And the unclean spirit threw him into convulsions, shouted with a loud voice, and came out of him.

[27] They were all amazed, and so they began to ask each other, "What is this? A new teaching with authority!

He commands even the unclean spirits, and they obey him."

[28] At once the news about him spread throughout the entire vicinity of Galilee.

Healings at Capernaum

SEE MT 8:14–17; LK 4:38–41

[29] As soon as they left the synagogue, they went into Simon and Andrew's house with James and John. [30] Simon's mother-in-law was lying in bed with a fever, and they told him about her at once. [31] So he went to her, took her by the hand, and raised her up. The fever left her, and she began to serve them.

[32] When evening came, after the sun had set, they brought to him all those who were sick and demon-possessed. [33] The whole town was assembled at the door, [34] and he healed many who were sick with various diseases and drove out many demons. And he would not permit the demons to speak, because they knew him.

Preaching in Galilee

SEE LK 4:42–43

[35] Very early in the morning, while it was still dark, he got up, went out, and made his way to a deserted place; and there he was praying. [36] Simon and his companions searched for him, [37] and when they found him they said, "Everyone is looking for you."

[38] And he said to them, "Let's go on to the neighboring villages so that I may preach there too. This is why I have come."

A Man Cleansed

SEE MT 8:1–4; LK 5:12–16

SEE MT 4:23–25; LK 4:44

[39] He went into all of Galilee, preaching in their synagogues and driving out demons. [40] Then a man with leprosy came to him and, on his knees, begged him, "If you are willing, you can make me clean." [41] Moved with compassion, Jesus reached out his hand and touched him. "I am willing," he told him. "Be made clean." [42] Immediately the leprosy left him, and he was made clean. [43] Then he sternly warned him and sent him away at once, [44] telling him, "See that you say nothing to anyone; but go and show yourself to the priest, and offer what Moses commanded for your cleansing, as a testimony to them." [45] Yet he went out and began to proclaim it widely and to spread the news, with the result that Jesus could no longer enter a town openly. But he was out in deserted places, and they came to him from everywhere.

Mark 2

The Son of Man Forgives and Heals

[1] When he entered Capernaum again after some days, it was reported that he was at home. [2] So many people gathered together that there was no more room, not even in the doorway, and he was speaking the word to them. [3] They came to him bringing a paralytic, carried by four of them. [4] Since they were not able to bring him to Jesus because of the crowd, they removed the roof above him, and after digging through it, they lowered the mat on which the paralytic was lying. [5] Seeing their faith, Jesus told the paralytic, "Son, your sins are forgiven."

[6] But some of the scribes were sitting there, questioning in their hearts: [7] "Why does he speak like this? He's blaspheming! Who can forgive sins but God alone?"

[8] Right away Jesus perceived in his spirit that they were thinking like this within themselves and said to them, "Why are you thinking these things in your hearts? [9] Which is easier: to say to the paralytic, 'Your sins are forgiven,' or to say, 'Get up, take your mat, and walk'? [10] But so that you may know that the Son of Man has authority on earth to forgive sins"—he told the paralytic— [11] "I tell you: get up, take your mat, and go home."

[12] Immediately he got up, took the mat, and went out in front of everyone. As a result, they were all astounded and gave glory to God, saying,

"We have never seen anything like this!"

SEE MT 9:1–8; LK 5:17–26

SEE MT 9:9–13; LK 5:27–32

The Call of Levi

¹³ Jesus went out again beside the sea. The whole crowd was coming to him, and he was teaching them. ¹⁴ Then, passing by, he saw Levi the son of Alphaeus sitting at the tax office, and he said to him, "Follow me," and he got up and followed him.

¹⁵ While he was reclining at the table in Levi's house, many tax collectors and sinners were eating with Jesus and his disciples, for there were many who were following him. ¹⁶ When the scribes who were Pharisees saw that he was eating with sinners and tax collectors, they asked his disciples, "Why does he eat with tax collectors and sinners?"

¹⁷ When Jesus heard this, he told them, "It is not those who are well who need a doctor, but those who are sick. I didn't come to call the righteous, but sinners."

SEE MT 9:14–17; LK 5:33–39

A Question About Fasting

¹⁸ Now John's disciples and the Pharisees were fasting. People came and asked him, "Why do John's disciples and the Pharisees' disciples fast, but your disciples do not fast?"

¹⁹ Jesus said to them, "The wedding guests cannot fast while the groom is with them, can they? As long as they have the groom with them, they cannot fast. ²⁰ But the time will come when the groom will be taken away from them, and then they will fast on that day. ²¹ No one sews a patch of unshrunk cloth on an old garment. Otherwise, the new patch pulls away from the old cloth, and a worse tear is made. ²² And no one puts new wine into old wineskins. Otherwise, the wine will burst the skins, and the wine is lost as well as the skins. No, new wine is put into fresh wineskins."

SEE MT 12:1–8; LK 6:1–5

Lord of the Sabbath

²³ On the Sabbath he was going through the grainfields, and his disciples began to make their way, picking some heads of grain. ²⁴ The Pharisees said to him, "Look, why are they doing what is not lawful on the Sabbath?"

²⁵ He said to them, "Have you never read what David and those who were with him did when he was in need and hungry— ²⁶ how he entered the house of God in the time of Abiathar the high priest and ate the bread of the Presence—which is not lawful for anyone to eat except the priests—and also gave some to his companions?" ²⁷ Then he told them, "The Sabbath was made for man and not man for the Sabbath. ²⁸ So then, the Son of Man is Lord even of the Sabbath."

DATE   /   /

SUMMARIZE TODAY'S READING.

WHAT IS SOMETHING I LEARNED OR WAS REMINDED OF ABOUT JESUS?

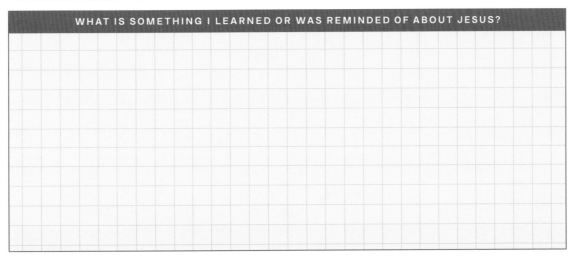

WHAT DID I NOTICE ABOUT THE WAY JESUS LIVED HIS LIFE?

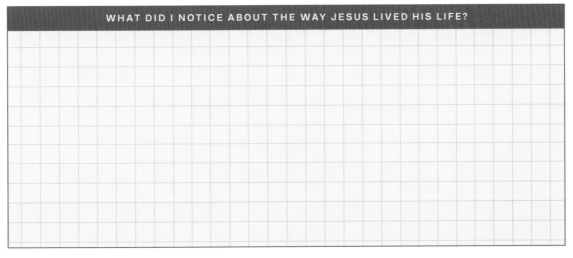

Jesus Teaches the Crowds

---

*"Blessed are those who hunger and
thirst for righteousness, for they will be filled."*

MATTHEW 5:6

Matthew 5:1–11

Ministry in Galilee

When he saw the crowds, he went up on the mountain, and after he sat down, his disciples came to him. ² Then he began to teach them, saying:

The Beatitudes

³ "Blessed are the poor in spirit,
for the kingdom of heaven is theirs.
⁴ Blessed are those who mourn,
for they will be comforted.
⁵ Blessed are the humble,
for they will inherit the earth.
⁶ Blessed are those who hunger and thirst
    for righteousness,
for they will be filled.
⁷ Blessed are the merciful,
for they will be shown mercy.
⁸ Blessed are the pure in heart,
for they will see God.
⁹ Blessed are the peacemakers,
for they will be called sons of God.
¹⁰ Blessed are those who are persecuted because
    of righteousness,
for the kingdom of heaven is theirs.

¹¹ "You are blessed when they insult you and persecute you and falsely say every kind of evil against you because of me."

Luke 6:20–26

The Beatitudes

²⁰ Then looking up at his disciples, he said:

Blessed are you who are poor,
because the kingdom of God is yours.
²¹ Blessed are you who are hungry now,
because you will be filled.
Blessed are you who weep now,
because you will laugh.
²² Blessed are you when people hate you,
when they exclude you, insult you,
and slander your name as evil
because of the Son of Man.

²³ "Rejoice in that day and leap for joy. Take note—your reward is great in heaven, for this is the way their ancestors used to treat the prophets.

Woe to the Self-Satisfied

²⁴ But woe to you who are rich,
for you have received your comfort.
²⁵ Woe to you who are now full,
for you will be hungry.
Woe to you who are now laughing,
for you will mourn and weep.
²⁶ Woe to you
when all people speak well of you,
for this is the way their ancestors
used to treat the false prophets."

Matthew 5:13–20

Believers Are Salt and Light

13 "You are the salt of the earth. But if the salt should lose its taste, how can it be made salty? It's no longer good for anything but to be thrown out and trampled under people's feet.

14 "You are the light of the world. A city situated on a hill cannot be hidden. 15 No one lights a lamp and puts it under a basket, but rather on a lampstand, and it gives light for all who are in the house. 16 In the same way,

let your light shine before others, so that they may see your good works and give glory to your Father in heaven.

Christ Fulfills the Law

17 "Don't think that I came to abolish the Law or the Prophets. I did not come to abolish but to fulfill. 18 For truly I tell you, until heaven and earth pass away, not the smallest letter or one stroke of a letter will pass away from the law until all things are accomplished. 19 Therefore, whoever breaks one of the least of these commands and teaches others to do the same will be called least in the kingdom of heaven. But whoever does and teaches these commands will be called great in the kingdom of heaven. 20 For I tell you, unless your righteousness surpasses that of the scribes and Pharisees, you will never get into the kingdom of heaven."

Matthew 6:1–4

How to Give

1 "Be careful not to practice your righteousness in front of others to be seen by them. Otherwise, you have no reward with your Father in heaven. 2 So whenever you give to the poor, don't sound a trumpet before you, as the hypocrites do in the synagogues and on the streets, to be applauded by people. Truly I tell you, they have their reward. 3 But when you give to the poor, don't let your left hand know what your right hand is doing, 4 so that your giving may be in secret. And your Father who sees in secret will reward you."

Matthew 7:7–12, 24–29

Ask, Search, Knock

7 "Ask, and it will be given to you. Seek, and you will find. Knock, and the door will be opened to you. 8 For everyone who asks receives, and the one who seeks finds, and to the one who knocks, the door will be opened. 9 Who among you, if his son asks him for bread, will give him a stone? 10 Or if he asks for a fish, will give him a snake? 11 If you then, who are evil, know how to give good gifts to your children, how much more will your Father in heaven give good things to those who ask him. 12 Therefore, whatever you want others to do for you, do also the same for them, for this is the Law and the Prophets."

…

The Two Foundations

24 "Therefore, everyone who hears these words of mine and acts on them will be like a wise man who built his house on the rock. 25 The rain fell, the rivers rose, and the winds blew and pounded that house. Yet it didn't collapse, because its foundation was on the rock. 26 But everyone who hears these words of mine and doesn't act on them will be like a foolish man who built his house on the sand. 27 The rain fell, the rivers rose, the winds blew and pounded that house, and it collapsed. It collapsed with a great crash."

28 When Jesus had finished saying these things, the crowds were astonished at his teaching, 29 because he was teaching them like one who had authority, and not like their scribes.

SEE LK 11:9–13

SEE LK 6:46–49

DATE   /   /

SUMMARIZE TODAY'S READING.

WHAT IS SOMETHING I LEARNED OR WAS REMINDED OF ABOUT JESUS?

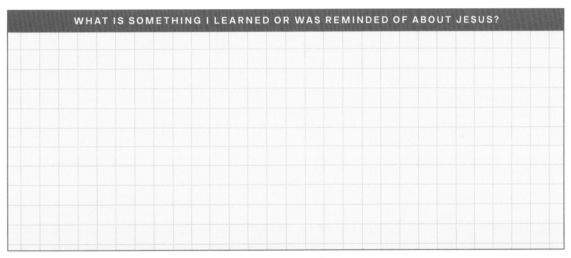

WHAT DID I NOTICE ABOUT THE WAY JESUS LIVED HIS LIFE?

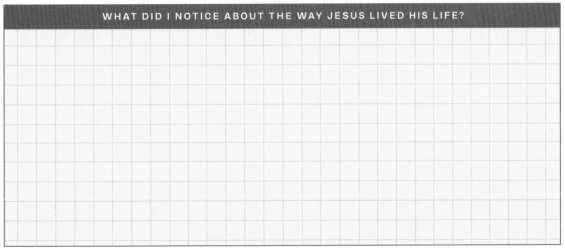

Jesus Teaches on Love and Forgiveness

"Her many sins have been forgiven; that's why she loved much."

LUKE 7:47

WEEK 02

DAY 10

Luke 7

A Centurion's Faith

SEE MT 8:5–13

When he had concluded saying all this to the people who were listening, he entered Capernaum. ² A centurion's servant, who was highly valued by him, was sick and about to die. ³ When the centurion heard about Jesus, he sent some Jewish elders to him, requesting him to come and save the life of his servant. ⁴ When they reached Jesus, they pleaded with him earnestly, saying, "He is worthy for you to grant this, ⁵ because he loves our nation and has built us a synagogue."

⁶ Jesus went with them, and when he was not far from the house, the centurion sent friends to tell him, "Lord, don't trouble yourself, since I am not worthy to have you come under my roof. ⁷ That is why I didn't even consider myself worthy to come to you. But say the word, and my servant will be healed. ⁸ For I too am a man placed under authority, having soldiers under my command. I say to this one, 'Go,' and he goes; and to another, 'Come,' and he comes; and to my servant, 'Do this,' and he does it."

⁹ Jesus heard this and was amazed at him, and turning to the crowd following him, he said, "I tell you, I have not found so great a faith even in Israel." ¹⁰ When those who had been sent returned to the house, they found the servant in good health.

A Widow's Son Raised to Life

¹¹ Afterward he was on his way to a town called Nain. His disciples and a large crowd were traveling with him. ¹² Just as he neared the gate of the town, a dead man was being carried out. He was his mother's only son, and she was a widow. A large crowd from the town was also with her. ¹³ When the Lord saw her, he had compassion on her and said, "Don't weep." ¹⁴ Then he came up and touched the open coffin, and the pallbearers stopped. And he said, "Young man, I tell you, get up!"

SEE MT 11:2–19

[15] The dead man sat up and began to speak, and Jesus gave him to his mother. [16] Then fear came over everyone, and they glorified God, saying, "A great prophet has risen among us," and "God has visited his people." [17] This report about him went throughout Judea and all the vicinity.

In Praise of John the Baptist

[18] Then John's disciples told him about all these things. So John summoned two of his disciples [19] and sent them to the Lord, asking, "Are you the one who is to come, or should we expect someone else?"

[20] When the men reached him, they said, "John the Baptist sent us to ask you, 'Are you the one who is to come, or should we expect someone else?'"

[21] At that time Jesus healed many people of diseases, afflictions, and evil spirits, and he granted sight to many blind people. [22] He replied to them, "Go and report to John what you have seen and heard: The blind receive their sight, the lame walk, those with leprosy are cleansed, the deaf hear, the dead are raised, and the poor are told the good news, [23] and blessed is the one who isn't offended by me."

[24] After John's messengers left, he began to speak to the crowds about John: "What did you go out into the wilderness to see? A reed swaying in the wind? [25] What then did you go out to see? A man dressed in soft clothes? See, those who are splendidly dressed and live in luxury are in royal palaces. [26] What then did you go out to see? A prophet? Yes, I tell you, and more than a prophet. [27] This is the one about whom it is written:

> See, I am sending my messenger
> ahead of you;
> he will prepare your way before you.

[28] I tell you, among those born of women no one is greater than John, but the least in the kingdom of God is greater than he."

²⁹ (And when all the people, including the tax collectors, heard this, they acknowledged God's way of righteousness, because they had been baptized with John's baptism. ³⁰ But since the Pharisees and experts in the law had not been baptized by him, they rejected the plan of God for themselves.)

An Unresponsive Generation

³¹ "To what then should I compare the people of this generation, and what are they like? ³² They are like children sitting in the marketplace and calling to each other:

We played the flute for you,
but you didn't dance;
we sang a lament,
but you didn't weep!

³³ For John the Baptist did not come eating bread or drinking wine, and you say, 'He has a demon!' ³⁴ The Son of Man has come eating and drinking, and you say, 'Look, a glutton and a drunkard, a friend of tax collectors and sinners!' ³⁵ Yet wisdom is vindicated by all her children."

Much Forgiveness, Much Love

³⁶ Then one of the Pharisees invited him to eat with him. He entered the Pharisee's house and reclined at the table. ³⁷ And a woman in the town who was a sinner found out that Jesus was reclining at the table in the Pharisee's house. She brought an alabaster jar of perfume ³⁸ and stood behind him at his feet, weeping, and began to wash his feet with her tears. She wiped his feet with her hair, kissing them and anointing them with the perfume.

³⁹ When the Pharisee who had invited him saw this, he said to himself, "This man, if he were a prophet, would know who and what kind of woman this is who is touching him—she's a sinner!"

NOTES

[40] Jesus replied to him, "Simon, I have something to say to you."

He said, "Say it, teacher."

[41] "A creditor had two debtors. One owed five hundred denarii, and the other fifty. [42] Since they could not pay it back, he graciously forgave them both. So, which of them will love him more?"

[43] Simon answered, "I suppose the one he forgave more."

"You have judged correctly," he told him. [44] Turning to the woman, he said to Simon, "Do you see this woman? I entered your house; you gave me no water for my feet, but she, with her tears, has washed my feet and wiped them with her hair. [45] You gave me no kiss, but she hasn't stopped kissing my feet since I came in. [46] You didn't anoint my head with olive oil, but she has anointed my feet with perfume. [47] Therefore I tell you, her many sins have been forgiven; that's why she loved much. But the one who is forgiven little, loves little." [48] Then he said to her, "Your sins are forgiven."

[49] Those who were at the table with him began to say among themselves, "Who is this man who even forgives sins?"

[50] And he said to the woman, "Your faith has saved you. Go in peace."

DATE   /   /

SUMMARIZE TODAY'S READING.

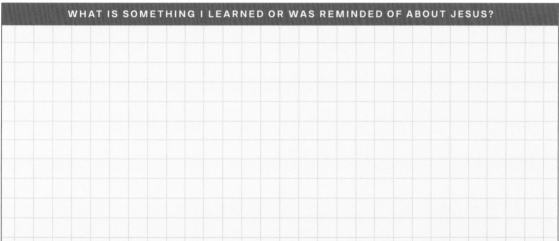

WHAT IS SOMETHING I LEARNED OR WAS REMINDED OF ABOUT JESUS?

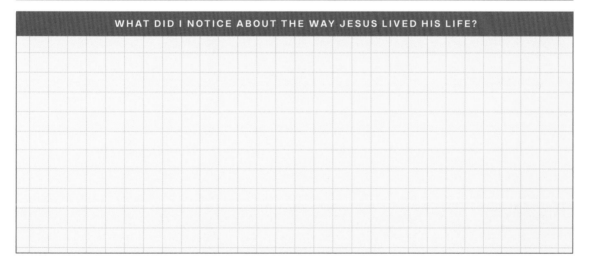

WHAT DID I NOTICE ABOUT THE WAY JESUS LIVED HIS LIFE?

Key Groups in the Gospels

—

In the Gospel accounts, we discover that Jesus was an individual who lived in the world with other people—He did not live in isolation. He encountered politicians, faith leaders, military personnel, financial workers, and others living their everyday lives. We learn more about who Jesus is when we observe how He interacted with diverse people groups. On the following pages you will find a list of each of the key groups named in the Gospels, along with a brief description of each group.

Centurions

MT 27:54; LK 7:2–3, 6; 23:47

· Professional commanding officers in the Roman army

· Had military experience, formal education, and respect in the public eye

· Commanded roughly eighty soldiers

Elders of the People

MT 21:23; MK 8:31; 14:53; LK 7:3; 22:52, 66

· A council of men from prominent Jewish families

· Held leadership role in the government of the local synagogue

· Part of the Sanhedrin

Gentiles

MT 4:15; LK 2:32; 18:32; 22:25

· All non-Jewish people and people groups

· Considered by Jewish people to be ceremonially unclean and outsiders to God's covenant and promise

Herodians

MT 22:16

· Jewish people who supported King Herod, who ruled Judea under the authority of the Roman Empire

· Joined with Pharisees in a plot to kill Jesus

· Tried to trick Jesus into saying people shouldn't pay taxes

Jews

MT 2:2; MK 15:18; LK 23:3, 37–38

· Descendants of Abraham

· Believers in the God of Abraham, Isaac, and Jacob

Money Changers

MT 21:12

· Responsible for exchanging other currencies for Jewish money

· Set up tables in the temple so worshipers could get the correct currency to pay the temple tax and buy sacrifices

· Often profited greatly by charging high interest rates

Pharisees

MT 5:20; 9:34; 21:45; 22:15, 34, 41; 23:2, 13, 15, 23, 25–27, 29; MK 2:16, 18, 24; 8:11, 15; LK 7:30, 36–37, 39; 15:2; 16:14

· "Set apart ones" focused on the study and interpretation of the law of Moses

· Believed both the written Law and oral tradition were authoritative for Jewish practice

· Led the local synagogues and had a strong influence in the Jewish community

Priests / Chief Priests / High Priests

MT 2:4; 21:15, 23, 45; 26:14; MK 1:44; 2:26; 8:31; 14:53–55, 60–61, 63; LK 1:5, 8–9; 3:2; 22:2–3, 50, 52, 54, 66; 23:4, 10, 13; 24:20

· Official worship leaders for the Jewish people

· Represented Israel before God and offered sacrifices on behalf of the people

· The most powerful Jewish people in Jerusalem

Sadducees

MT 22:23, 34

- Wealthy high priests who were politically oriented

- "Righteous ones" focused on maintaining the beliefs and practices of the past

- Did not believe in the resurrection of the dead and denied the existence of demons and angels

The Sanhedrin

MK 14:55; LK 22:66; 23:50

- A seventy-one-member Jewish council in Jerusalem, run by the high priest

- Made up of Sadducees, Pharisees, priests, and elders of the people

- Had local authority over the Jewish community under Roman oversight

Scribes

MT 2:4; 5:20; 7:29; 17:10; 21:15; 23:2, 13, 15, 23, 25, 27, 29, 34; MK 2:6, 16; 8:31; 12:38; 14:53; LK 15:2; 22:2, 66; 23:10

- Religious group trained in interpreting the law of Moses

- Largely made up of Pharisees

Tax Collectors

MT 10:3; 18:17; 21:31–32; MK 2:15–16; LK 3:12; 7:29, 34; 15:1; 19:2

- Hired by contract from the Roman government to collect taxes

- Collected additional profit with the taxes for their pay

- Were regarded as treasonous, greedy, and dishonest by fellow Jewish people

Zealots

MT 10:4

- An extreme political sect of Pharisees committed to resisting Rome

- Believed only God had the right to rule the Jewish people and were willing to die for that belief

- Considered their patriotism and religious beliefs to be inseparable

Jesus Begins to
Teach in Parables

"Let anyone who has ears to hear listen."

MARK 4:9

Mark 4

The Parable of the Sower

Again he began to teach by the sea, and a very large crowd gathered around him. So he got into a boat on the sea and sat down, while the whole crowd was by the sea on the shore.

² He taught them many things in parables,

and in his teaching he said to them, ³ "Listen! Consider the sower who went out to sow. ⁴ As he sowed, some seed fell along the path, and the birds came and devoured it. ⁵ Other seed fell on rocky ground where it didn't have much soil, and it grew up quickly, since the soil wasn't deep. ⁶ When the sun came up, it was scorched, and since it had no root, it withered away. ⁷ Other seed fell among thorns, and the thorns came up and choked it, and it didn't produce fruit. ⁸ Still other seed fell on good ground and it grew up, producing fruit that increased thirty, sixty, and a hundred times." ⁹ Then he said, "Let anyone who has ears to hear listen."

Why Jesus Used Parables

¹⁰ When he was alone, those around him with the Twelve asked him about the parables. ¹¹ He answered them, "The secret of the kingdom of God has been given to you, but to those outside, everything comes in parables ¹² so that

they may indeed look,
and yet not perceive;
they may indeed listen,
and yet not understand;
otherwise, they might turn back
and be forgiven."

The Parable of the Sower Explained

¹³ Then he said to them, "Don't you understand this parable? How then will you understand all of the parables? ¹⁴ The sower sows the word. ¹⁵ Some are like the word sown on the path. When they hear, immediately Satan comes and takes away the word sown in them. ¹⁶ And others are like seed sown on rocky ground. When they hear the word, immediately they receive it with joy. ¹⁷ But they have no root; they are short-lived. When distress or persecution comes because of the word, they immediately fall away. ¹⁸ Others are like seed sown among thorns; these are the ones who hear the word, ¹⁹ but the worries of this age, the deceitfulness of wealth, and the desires for other things enter in and choke the word, and it becomes unfruitful. ²⁰ And those like seed sown on good ground hear the word, welcome it, and produce fruit thirty, sixty, and a hundred times what was sown."

SEE MT 13:1–23; LK 8:4–15

Using Your Light

SEE LK 8:16-18

[21] He also said to them, "Is a lamp brought in to be put under a basket or under a bed? Isn't it to be put on a lampstand? [22] For there is nothing hidden that will not be revealed, and nothing concealed that will not be brought to light. [23] If anyone has ears to hear, let him listen." [24] And he said to them, "Pay attention to what you hear. By the measure you use, it will be measured to you—and more will be added to you. [25] For whoever has, more will be given to him, and whoever does not have, even what he has will be taken away from him."

The Parable of the Growing Seed

[26] "The kingdom of God is like this," he said. "A man scatters seed on the ground. [27] He sleeps and rises night and day; the seed sprouts and grows, although he doesn't know how. [28] The soil produces a crop by itself—first the blade, then the head, and then the full grain on the head. [29] As soon as the crop is ready, he sends for the sickle, because the harvest has come."

The Parable of the Mustard Seed

SEE MT 13:31-35

[30] And he said, "With what can we compare the kingdom of God, or what parable can we use to describe it? [31] It's like a mustard seed that, when sown upon the soil, is the smallest of all the seeds on the ground. [32] And when sown, it comes up and grows taller than all the garden plants, and produces large branches, so that the birds of the sky can nest in its shade."

Using Parables

[33] He was speaking the word to them with many parables like these, as they were able to understand. [34] He did not speak to them without a parable. Privately, however, he explained everything to his own disciples.

Wind and Waves Obey Jesus

SEE MT 8:23-27; LK 8:22-25

[35] On that day, when evening had come, he told them, "Let's cross over to the other side of the sea." [36] So they left the crowd and took him along since he was in the boat. And other boats were with him. [37] A great windstorm arose, and the waves were breaking over the boat, so that the boat was already being swamped. [38] He was in the stern, sleeping on the cushion. So they woke him up and said to him, "Teacher! Don't you care that we're going to die?"

[39] He got up, rebuked the wind, and said to the sea, "Silence! Be still!" The wind ceased, and there was a great calm. [40] Then he said to them, "Why are you afraid? Do you still have no faith?"

[41] And they were terrified and asked one another, "Who then is this? Even the wind and the sea obey him!"

DATE   /   /

SUMMARIZE TODAY'S READING.

WHAT IS SOMETHING I LEARNED OR WAS REMINDED OF ABOUT JESUS?

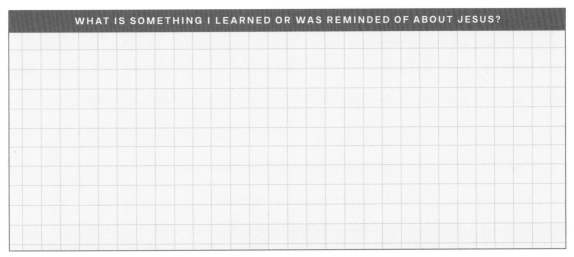

WHAT DID I NOTICE ABOUT THE WAY JESUS LIVED HIS LIFE?

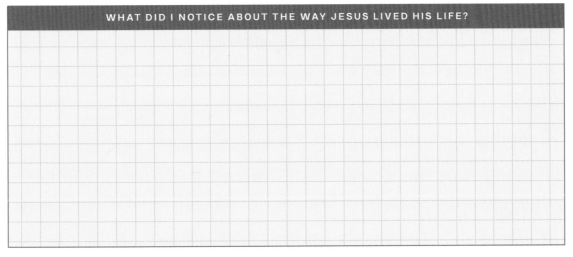

Jesus Heals and Performs Miracles

"Daughter," he said to her, "your faith has saved you. Go in peace."

LUKE 8:48

Luke 8:26–56

Demons Driven Out by Jesus

SEE MT 8:28–34; MK 5:1–20

[26] Then they sailed to the region of the Gerasenes, which is opposite Galilee. [27] When he got out on land, a demon-possessed man from the town met him. For a long time he had worn no clothes and did not stay in a house but in the tombs. [28] When he saw Jesus, he cried out, fell down before him, and said in a loud voice, "What do you have to do with me, Jesus, Son of the Most High God? I beg you, don't torment me!" [29] For he had commanded the unclean spirit to come out of the man. Many times it had seized him, and though he was guarded, bound by chains and shackles, he would snap the restraints and be driven by the demon into deserted places.

[30] "What is your name?" Jesus asked him.

"Legion," he said, because many demons had entered him. [31] And they begged him not to banish them to the abyss.

[32] A large herd of pigs was there, feeding on the hillside. The demons begged him to permit them to enter the pigs, and he gave them permission. [33] The demons came out of the man and entered the pigs, and the herd rushed down the steep bank into the lake and drowned.

[34] When the men who tended them saw what had happened, they ran off and reported it in the town and in the countryside. [35] Then people went out to see what had happened. They came to Jesus and found the man the demons had departed from, sitting at Jesus's feet, dressed and in his right mind. And they were afraid. [36] Meanwhile, the eyewitnesses reported to them how the demon-possessed man was delivered. [37] Then all the people of the Gerasene region asked him to leave them, because they were gripped by great fear. So getting into the boat, he returned.

[38] The man from whom the demons had departed begged him earnestly to be with him. But he sent him away and said,

[39] **"Go back to your home, and tell all that God has done for you."**

And off he went, proclaiming throughout the town how much Jesus had done for him.

SEE MT 9:18–26; MK 5:21–43

A Girl Restored and a Woman Healed

40 When Jesus returned, the crowd welcomed him, for they were all expecting him. 41 Just then, a man named Jairus came. He was a leader of the synagogue. He fell down at Jesus's feet and pleaded with him to come to his house, 42 because he had an only daughter about twelve years old, and she was dying.

While he was going, the crowds were nearly crushing him. 43 A woman suffering from bleeding for twelve years, who had spent all she had on doctors and yet could not be healed by any, 44 approached from behind and touched the end of his robe. Instantly her bleeding stopped.

45 "Who touched me?" Jesus asked.

When they all denied it, Peter said, "Master, the crowds are hemming you in and pressing against you."

46 "Someone did touch me," said Jesus. "I know that power has gone out from me." 47 When the woman saw that she was discovered, she came trembling and fell down before him. In the presence of all the people, she declared the reason she had touched him and how she was instantly healed. 48 "Daughter," he said to her, "your faith has saved you. Go in peace."

49 While he was still speaking, someone came from the synagogue leader's house and said, "Your daughter is dead. Don't bother the teacher anymore."

50 When Jesus heard it, he answered him, "Don't be afraid. Only believe, and she will be saved." 51 After he came to the house, he let no one enter with him except Peter, John, James, and the child's father and mother. 52 Everyone was crying and mourning for her. But he said, "Stop crying, because she is not dead but asleep."

53 They laughed at him, because they knew she was dead. 54 So he took her by the hand and called out, "Child, get up!" 55 Her spirit returned, and she got up at once. Then he gave orders that she be given something to eat. 56 Her parents were astounded, but he instructed them to tell no one what had happened.

Matthew 9:27–38

Healing the Blind

27 As Jesus went on from there, two blind men followed him, calling out, "Have mercy on us, Son of David!"

28 When he entered the house, the blind men approached him, and Jesus said to them, "Do you believe that I can do this?"

They said to him, "Yes, Lord."

29 Then he touched their eyes, saying, "Let it be done for you according to your faith." 30 And their eyes were opened. Then Jesus warned them sternly, "Be sure that no one finds out." 31 But they went out and spread the news about him throughout that whole area.

Driving Out a Demon

32 Just as they were going out, a demon-possessed man who was unable to speak was brought to him. 33 When the demon had been driven out, the man who had been mute spoke, and the crowds were amazed, saying, "Nothing like this has ever been seen in Israel!"

34 But the Pharisees said, "He drives out demons by the ruler of the demons."

The Lord of the Harvest

35 Jesus continued going around to all the towns and villages, teaching in their synagogues, preaching the good news of the kingdom, and healing every disease and every sickness. 36 When he saw the crowds, he felt compassion for them, because they were distressed and dejected, like sheep without a shepherd. 37 Then he said to his disciples, "The harvest is abundant, but the workers are few. 38 Therefore, pray to the Lord of the harvest to send out workers into his harvest."

DATE   /   /

SUMMARIZE TODAY'S READING.

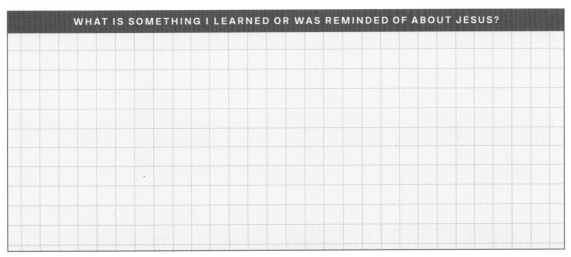

WHAT IS SOMETHING I LEARNED OR WAS REMINDED OF ABOUT JESUS?

WHAT DID I NOTICE ABOUT THE WAY JESUS LIVED HIS LIFE?

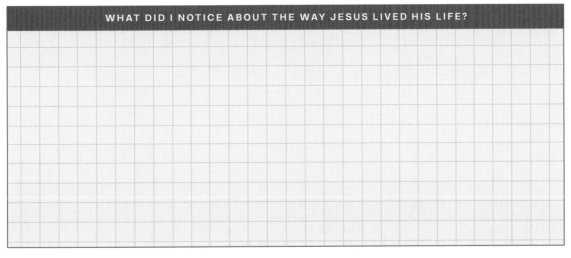

Grace Day

Take this day to catch up on your reading, pray, and rest in the presence of the Lord.

Matthew

"Ask, and it will
be given to you.
Seek, and you will
find. Knock, and the
door will be opened to
you. For everyone who
asks receives, and the one
who seeks finds, and to
the one who knocks, the
door will be opened."

Matthew 7:7-8

Seek...

Weekly Truth

Scripture is God-breathed and true. When we memorize it,
we carry the good news of Jesus with us wherever we go.

This week we will continue memorizing our key passage
by adding the next section of verse 35.

Jesus continued going around to all the towns and villages, teaching in their synagogues, preaching the good news of the kingdom, and healing every disease and every sickness. When he saw the crowds, he felt compassion for them, because they were distressed and dejected, like sheep without a shepherd.

MATTHEW 9:35–36

See tips for memorizing Scripture on page 188.

Jesus Feeds the Five Thousand

He saw a large crowd and had compassion on them.

MARK 6:34

Matthew 10:1–4

Commissioning the Twelve

Summoning his twelve disciples, he gave them authority over unclean spirits, to drive them out and to heal every disease and sickness. [2] These are the names of the twelve apostles: First, Simon, who is called Peter, and Andrew his brother; James the son of Zebedee, and John his brother; [3] Philip and Bartholomew; Thomas and Matthew the tax collector; James the son of Alphaeus, and Thaddaeus; [4] Simon the Zealot, and Judas Iscariot, who also betrayed him.

Mark 6:7–56

Commissioning the Twelve

[7] He summoned the Twelve and began to send them out in pairs and gave them authority over unclean spirits. [8] He instructed them to take nothing for the road except a staff—no bread, no traveling bag, no money in their belts, [9] but to wear sandals and not put on an extra shirt. [10] He said to them, "Whenever you enter a house, stay there until you leave that place. [11] If any place does not welcome you or listen to you, when you leave there, shake the dust off your feet as a testimony against them." [12] So they went out and preached that people should repent. [13] They drove out many demons, anointed many sick people with oil and healed them.

John the Baptist Beheaded

[14] King Herod heard about it, because Jesus's name had become well known. Some said, "John the Baptist has been raised from the dead, and that's why miraculous powers are at work in him." [15] But others said, "He's Elijah." Still others said, "He's a prophet, like one of the prophets from long ago."

[16] When Herod heard of it, he said, "John, the one I beheaded, has been raised!"

[17] For Herod himself had given orders to arrest John and to chain him in prison on account of Herodias, his brother Philip's wife, because he had married her. [18] John had been telling Herod, "It is not lawful for

SEE MT 10:5–15; LK 9:3–6

SEE MT 14:1–2; LK 9:7–9

you to have your brother's wife." [19] So Herodias held a grudge against him and wanted to kill him. But she could not, [20] because Herod feared John and protected him, knowing he was a righteous and holy man. When Herod heard him he would be very perplexed, and yet he liked to listen to him.

[21] An opportune time came on his birthday, when Herod gave a banquet for his nobles, military commanders, and the leading men of Galilee. [22] When Herodias's own daughter came in and danced, she pleased Herod and his guests. The king said to the girl, "Ask me whatever you want, and I'll give it to you." [23] He promised her with an oath: "Whatever you ask me I will give you, up to half my kingdom."

[24] She went out and said to her mother, "What should I ask for?"

"John the Baptist's head," she said.

[25] At once she hurried to the king and said, "I want you to give me John the Baptist's head on a platter immediately." [26] Although the king was deeply distressed, because of his oaths and the guests he did not want to refuse her. [27] The king immediately sent for an executioner and commanded him to bring John's head. So he went and beheaded him in prison, [28] brought his head on a platter, and gave it to the girl. Then the girl gave it to her mother. [29] When John's disciples heard about it, they came and removed his corpse and placed it in a tomb.

Feeding of the Five Thousand

[30] The apostles gathered around Jesus and reported to him all that they had done and taught. [31] He said to them, "Come away by yourselves to a remote place and rest for a while." For many people were coming and going, and they did not even have time to eat.

[32] So they went away in the boat by themselves to a remote place, [33] but many saw them leaving and

SEE MT 14:13–21; LK 9:10–17

recognized them, and they ran on foot from all the towns and arrived ahead of them.

[34] When he went ashore, he saw a large crowd and had compassion on them, because they were like sheep without a shepherd. Then he began to teach them many things.

[35] When it grew late, his disciples approached him and said, "This place is deserted, and it is already late. [36] Send them away so that they can go into the surrounding countryside and villages to buy themselves something to eat."

[37] "You give them something to eat," he responded.

They said to him, "Should we go and buy two hundred denarii worth of bread and give them something to eat?"

[38] He asked them, "How many loaves do you have? Go and see."

When they found out they said, "Five, and two fish." [39] Then he instructed them to have all the people sit down in groups on the green grass. [40] So they sat down in groups of hundreds and fifties. [41] He took the five loaves and the two fish, and looking up to heaven, he blessed and broke the loaves. He kept giving them to his disciples to set before the people. He also divided the two fish among them all.

[42] Everyone ate and was satisfied.

[43] They picked up twelve baskets full of pieces of bread and fish. [44] Now those who had eaten the loaves were five thousand men.

SEE MT 14:22-36

Walking on the Water

[45] Immediately he made his disciples get into the boat and go ahead of him to the other side, to Bethsaida, while he dismissed the crowd. [46] After he said good-bye to them, he went away to the mountain to pray. [47] Well into the night, the boat was in the middle of the sea, and he was alone on the land. [48] He saw them straining at the oars, because the wind was against them. Very early in the morning he came toward them walking on the sea and wanted to pass by them. [49] When they saw him walking on the sea, they thought it was a ghost and cried out, [50] because they all saw him and were terrified. Immediately he spoke with them and said, "Have courage! It is I. Don't be afraid." [51] Then he got into the boat with them, and the wind ceased. They were completely astounded, [52] because they had not understood about the loaves. Instead, their hearts were hardened.

Miraculous Healings

[53] When they had crossed over, they came to shore at Gennesaret and anchored there.

[54] As they got out of the boat, people immediately recognized him. [55] They hurried throughout that region and began to carry the sick on mats to wherever they heard he was. [56] Wherever he went, into villages, towns, or the country, they laid the sick in the marketplaces and begged him that they might touch just the end of his robe. And everyone who touched it was healed.

DATE   /   /

WHAT IS SOMETHING I LEARNED OR WAS REMINDED OF ABOUT JESUS?

WHAT DID I NOTICE ABOUT THE WAY JESUS LIVED HIS LIFE?

Peter's Confession of the Messiah

You are the Messiah, the Son of the living God.

MATTHEW 16:16

long
distance

1.12.23

Mark 8:1–30

Feeding Four Thousand

SEE MT 15:32–39

In those days there was again a large crowd, and they had nothing to eat. He called the disciples and said to them, ² "I have compassion on the crowd, because they've already stayed with me three days and have nothing to eat. ³ If I send them home hungry, they will collapse on the way, and some of them have come a long distance."

⁴ His disciples answered him, "Where can anyone get enough bread here in this desolate place to feed these people?"

⁵ "How many loaves do you have?" he asked them.

"Seven," they said. ⁶ He commanded the crowd to sit down on the ground. Taking the seven loaves, he gave thanks, broke them, and gave them to his disciples to set before the people. So they served them to the crowd. ⁷ They also had a few small fish, and after he had blessed them, he said these were to be served as well. ⁸ They ate and were satisfied. Then they collected seven large baskets of leftover pieces. ⁹ About four thousand were there. He dismissed them. ¹⁰ And he immediately got into the boat with his disciples and went to the district of Dalmanutha.

SEE MT 16:1-12

The Leaven of the Pharisees and Herod

[11] The Pharisees came and began to argue with him, demanding of him a sign from heaven to test him. [12] Sighing deeply in his spirit, he said, "Why does this generation demand a sign? Truly I tell you, no sign will be given to this generation." [13] Then he left them, got back into the boat, and went to the other side.

[14] The disciples had forgotten to take bread and had only one loaf with them in the boat. [15] Then he gave them strict orders: "Watch out! Beware of the leaven of the Pharisees and the leaven of Herod." [16] They were discussing among themselves that they did not have any bread. [17] Aware of this, he said to them, "Why are you discussing the fact you have no bread? Don't you understand or comprehend? Do you have hardened hearts? [18] Do you have eyes and not see; do you have ears and not hear? And do you not remember? [19] When I broke the five loaves for the five thousand, how many baskets full of leftovers did you collect?"

"Twelve," they told him.

[20] "When I broke the seven loaves for the four thousand, how many baskets full of pieces did you collect?"

"Seven," they said.

[21] And he said to them, "Don't you understand yet?"

Healing a Blind Man

[22] They came to Bethsaida. They brought a blind man to him and begged him to touch him. [23] He took the blind man by the hand and brought him out of the village. Spitting on his eyes and laying his hands on him, he asked him, "Do you see anything?"

²⁴ He looked up and said, "I see people—they look like trees walking."

²⁵ Again Jesus placed his hands on the man's eyes. The man looked intently and his sight was restored and he saw everything clearly. ²⁶ Then he sent him home, saying, "Don't even go into the village."

Peter's Confession of the Messiah

²⁷ Jesus went out with his disciples to the villages of Caesarea Philippi. And on the road he asked his disciples, "Who do people say that I am?"

²⁸ They answered him, "John the Baptist; others, Elijah; still others, one of the prophets."

²⁹ "But you," he asked them, "who do you say that I am?"

Peter answered him, "You are the Messiah." ³⁰ And he strictly warned them to tell no one about him.

Matthew 16:13–20

Peter's Confession of the Messiah

¹³ When Jesus came to the region of Caesarea Philippi, he asked his disciples, "Who do people say that the Son of Man is?"

¹⁴ They replied, "Some say John the Baptist; others, Elijah; still others, Jeremiah or one of the prophets."

¹⁵ "But you," he asked them, "who do you say that I am?"

¹⁶ Simon Peter answered, "You are the Messiah, the Son of the living God."

[17] Jesus responded, "Blessed are you, Simon son of Jonah, because flesh and blood did not reveal this to you, but my Father in heaven. [18] And I also say to you that you are Peter, and on this rock I will build my church, and the gates of Hades will not overpower it. [19] I will give you the keys of the kingdom of heaven, and whatever you bind on earth will have been bound in heaven, and whatever you loose on earth will have been loosed in heaven." [20] Then he gave the disciples orders to tell no one that he was the Messiah.

Mark 8:31–38

His Death and Resurrection Predicted

[31] Then he began to teach them that it was necessary for the Son of Man to suffer many things and be rejected by the elders, chief priests, and scribes, be killed, and rise after three days. [32] He spoke openly about this. Peter took him aside and began to rebuke him. [33] But turning around and looking at his disciples, he rebuked Peter and said, "Get behind me, Satan! You are not thinking about God's concerns but human concerns."

Take Up Your Cross

[34] Calling the crowd along with his disciples, he said to them, "If anyone wants to follow after me, let him deny himself, take up his cross, and follow me. [35] For whoever wants to save his life will lose it, but whoever loses his life because of me and the gospel will save it. [36] For what does it benefit someone to gain the whole world and yet lose his life? [37] What can anyone give in exchange for his life? [38] For whoever is ashamed of me and my words in this adulterous and sinful generation, the Son of Man will also be ashamed of him when he comes in the glory of his Father with the holy angels."

Mark 9:1

Then he said to them, "Truly I tell you, there are some standing here who will not taste death until they see the kingdom of God come in power."

SEE MT 16:21-27; LK 9:21-26

SEE MT 16:28; LK 9:27

DATE   /   /

SUMMARIZE TODAY'S READING.

WHAT IS SOMETHING I LEARNED OR WAS REMINDED OF ABOUT JESUS?

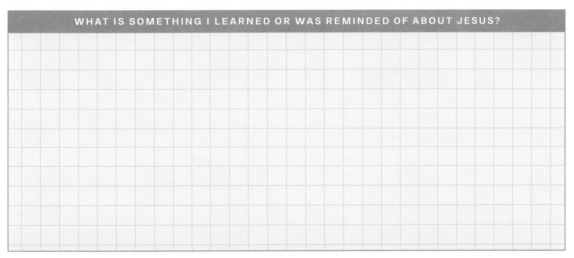

WHAT DID I NOTICE ABOUT THE WAY JESUS LIVED HIS LIFE?

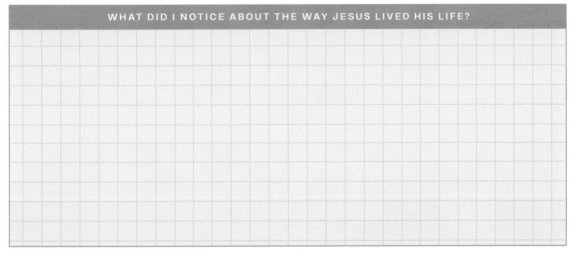

Who Is Jesus?

—

In Mark 8:27, Jesus asked His disciples, "Who do people say that I am?" When we look at the birth, life, ministry, death, and resurrection of Jesus as presented by the Gospel writers, we discover the depth and breadth of the answer. Here is a look at how the Gospels of Matthew, Mark, and Luke answer this question.

Characteristic	Matthew	Mark	Luke
JESUS IS THE SON OF GOD. Through the authors, the disciples, the Gentiles, and Jesus Himself, all four Gospels testify that Christ is the Son of God.	16:15–16; 27:54	1:1	22:70–71
JESUS IS GOD WHO TOOK ON HUMAN NATURE. Jesus is both fully God and fully human. The divinity and humanity of Jesus, which are both essential for His work as our Savior, are displayed through the testimony of the Gospel writers and the disciples. Some accounts highlight Jesus's humanity, others highlight His divinity, and some display the ever-present reality of His dual nature.	2:11	1:11	1:31–35
JESUS IS THE CHRIST, THE MESSIAH. Jesus is the Messiah—the Anointed One and promised deliverer of the nation of Israel and of all humanity.	26:63–64	8:27–29	2:11
JESUS CAME TO RELEASE SINNERS FROM CAPTIVITY. Jesus's purpose on earth was to conquer sin and evil, saving sinners by taking their punishment upon Himself. Only He can release us from the power and ultimate consequences of sin.	9:13	2:17	4:18–19

Characteristic	Matthew	Mark	Luke
JESUS HAS POWER TO FORGIVE SINS. Because He is God, Jesus has the authority to forgive sins.	9:1–8	2:9–12	24:47
JESUS HAS AUTHORITY OVER DEATH. Jesus has power to raise the dead, and He conquered death through His perfect life, sacrificial death, and glorious resurrection.	28:5–6	5:22–24, 35–42	24:5–6
JESUS HAS POWER TO GIVE ETERNAL LIFE. Jesus has authority to grant eternal life to all those who believe in Him.	25:45–46	10:29–30	23:43
JESUS CAME TO HEAL THE SICK AND SUFFERING . While on earth Jesus healed many people, from those with skin diseases and fevers to those blind and lame from birth.	8:5–13	1:32–34	5:12–15

Characteristic	Matthew	Mark	Luke
JESUS TAUGHT AND MINISTERED WITH AUTHORITY. As the Son of God, Jesus had and has authority over heaven and earth.	28:18	1:21–22	8:22–25
JESUS IS COMPASSIONATE TOWARD THE MARGINALIZED. Jesus showed compassion for all people—those who were lost and those who followed Him. He especially cared for those who were marginalized, outcast, or disenfranchised.	9:36	1:41	5:27–32
JESUS DEMONSTRATED A RANGE OF EMOTIONS. The Gospel accounts record Jesus experiencing sorrow, joy, anguish, anger, and many other emotions.	26:38	10:14	10:21
JESUS RESISTED TEMPTATION. Jesus lived His earthly life according to the truth of God and His Word, modeling obedience even through temptation.	4:1–11	14:36	23:46

The Transfiguration

His face shone like the sun; his clothes became as white as the light.

MATTHEW 17:2

WEEK 03   DAY 17

Matthew 17

The Transfiguration

After six days Jesus took Peter, James, and his brother John and led them up on a high mountain by themselves. [2] He was transfigured in front of them, and his face shone like the sun; his clothes became as white as the light. [3] Suddenly, Moses and Elijah appeared to them, talking with him. [4] Then Peter said to Jesus, "Lord, it's good for us to be here. If you want, I will set up three shelters here: one for you, one for Moses, and one for Elijah."

[5] While he was still speaking, suddenly a bright cloud covered them, and a voice from the cloud said, "This is my beloved Son, with whom I am well-pleased. Listen to him!" [6] When the disciples heard this, they fell facedown and were terrified.

[7] Jesus came up, touched them, and said, "Get up; don't be afraid." [8] When they looked up they saw no one except Jesus alone.

[9] As they were coming down the mountain, Jesus commanded them, "Don't tell anyone about the vision until the Son of Man is raised from the dead."

SEE MK 9:2–13; LK 9:28–36

[10] So the disciples asked him, "Why then do the scribes say that Elijah must come first?"

[11] "Elijah is coming and will restore everything," he replied. [12] "But I tell you: Elijah has already come, and they didn't recognize him. On the contrary, they did whatever they pleased to him. In the same way the Son of Man is going to suffer at their hands." [13] Then the disciples understood that he had spoken to them about John the Baptist.

The Power of Jesus over a Demon

[14] When they reached the crowd, a man approached and knelt down before him. [15] "Lord," he said, "have mercy on my son, because he has seizures and suffers terribly. He often falls into the fire and often into the water. [16] I brought him to your disciples, but they couldn't heal him."

[17] Jesus replied, "You unbelieving and perverse generation, how long will I be with you? How long must I put up with you? Bring him here to me." [18] Then Jesus rebuked the demon, and it came out of him, and from that moment the boy was healed.

[19] Then the disciples approached Jesus privately and said, "Why couldn't we drive it out?"

[20] "Because of your little faith," he told them. "For truly I tell you, if you have faith the size of a mustard seed, you will tell this mountain, 'Move from here to there,' and it will move. Nothing will be impossible for you."

The Second Prediction of His Death

[22] As they were gathering together in Galilee, Jesus told them, "The Son of Man is about to be betrayed into the hands of men. [23] They will kill him, and on the third day he will be raised up." And they were deeply distressed.

Paying the Temple Tax

[24] When they came to Capernaum, those who collected the temple tax approached Peter and said, "Doesn't your teacher pay the temple tax?"

[25] "Yes," he said.

SEE MK 9:14–32; LK 9:37–45

When he went into the house, Jesus spoke to him first, "What do you think, Simon? From whom do earthly kings collect tariffs or taxes? From their sons or from strangers?"

²⁶ "From strangers," he said.

"Then the sons are free," Jesus told him. ²⁷ "But, so we won't offend them, go to the sea, cast in a fishhook, and take the first fish that you catch. When you open its mouth you'll find a coin. Take it and give it to them for me and you."

Matthew 18

Who Is the Greatest?

¹ At that time the disciples came to Jesus and asked, "So who is greatest in the kingdom of heaven?" ² He called a small child and had him stand among them. ³ "Truly I tell you," he said, "unless you turn and become like little children, you will never enter the kingdom of heaven. ⁴ Therefore, whoever humbles himself like this child—this one is the greatest in the kingdom of heaven. ⁵ And whoever welcomes one child like this in my name welcomes me.

⁶ "But whoever causes one of these little ones who believe in me to fall away—it would be better for him if a heavy millstone were hung around his neck and he were drowned in the depths of the sea. ⁷ Woe to the world because of offenses. For offenses will inevitably come, but woe to that person by whom the offense comes. ⁸ If your hand or your foot causes you to fall away, cut it off and throw it away. It is better for you to enter life maimed or lame than to have two hands or two feet and be thrown into the eternal fire. ⁹ And if your eye causes you to fall away, gouge it out and throw it away. It is better for you to enter life with one eye than to have two eyes and be thrown into hellfire.

SEE MK 9:33–36; LK 9:46–47

SEE MK 9:37; LK 9:48

SEE MK 9:43–48

SEE MK 9:42

The Parable of the Lost Sheep

[10] "See to it that you don't despise one of these little ones, because I tell you that in heaven their angels continually view the face of my Father in heaven. [12] What do you think? If someone has a hundred sheep, and one of them goes astray, won't he leave the ninety-nine on the hillside and go and search for the stray? [13] And if he finds it, truly I tell you, he rejoices over that sheep more than over the ninety-nine that did not go astray. [14] In the same way, it is not the will of your Father in heaven that one of these little ones perish.

Restoring a Brother

[15] "If your brother sins against you, go tell him his fault, between you and him alone. If he listens to you, you have won your brother. [16] But if he won't listen, take one or two others with you, so that by the testimony of two or three witnesses every fact may be established. [17] If he doesn't pay attention to them, tell the church. If he doesn't pay attention even to the church, let him be like a Gentile and a tax collector to you. [18] Truly I tell you, whatever you bind on earth will have been bound in heaven, and whatever you loose on earth will have been loosed in heaven. [19] Again, truly I tell you, if two of you on earth agree about any matter that you pray for, it will be done for you by my Father in heaven. [20] For where two or three are gathered together in my name, I am there among them."

The Parable of the Unforgiving Servant

[21] Then Peter approached him and asked, "Lord, how many times must I forgive my brother or sister who sins against me? As many as seven times?"

[22] "I tell you, not as many as seven," Jesus replied, "but seventy times seven.

²³ "For this reason, the kingdom of heaven can be compared to a king who wanted to settle accounts with his servants. ²⁴ When he began to settle accounts, one who owed ten thousand talents was brought before him. ²⁵ Since he did not have the money to pay it back, his master commanded that he, his wife, his children, and everything he had be sold to pay the debt.

²⁶ "At this, the servant fell facedown before him and said, 'Be patient with me, and I will pay you everything.' ²⁷ Then the master of that servant had compassion, released him, and forgave him the loan.

²⁸ "That servant went out and found one of his fellow servants who owed him a hundred denarii. He grabbed him, started choking him, and said, 'Pay what you owe!'

²⁹ "At this, his fellow servant fell down and began begging him, 'Be patient with me, and I will pay you back.' ³⁰ But he wasn't willing. Instead, he went and threw him into prison until he could pay what was owed. ³¹ When the other servants saw what had taken place, they were deeply distressed and went and reported to their master everything that had happened. ³² Then, after he had summoned him, his master said to him, 'You wicked servant! I forgave you all that debt because you begged me. ³³ Shouldn't you also have had mercy on your fellow servant, as I had mercy on you?' ³⁴ And because he was angry, his master handed him over to the jailers to be tortured until he could pay everything that was owed. ³⁵ So also my heavenly Father will do to you unless every one of you forgives his brother or sister from your heart."

DATE   /   /

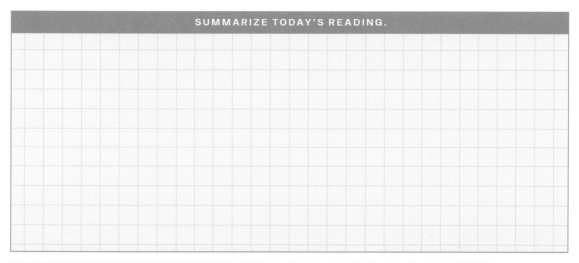

SUMMARIZE TODAY'S READING.

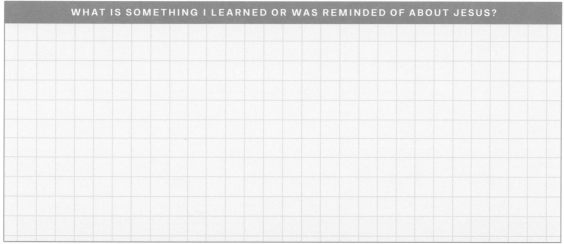

WHAT IS SOMETHING I LEARNED OR WAS REMINDED OF ABOUT JESUS?

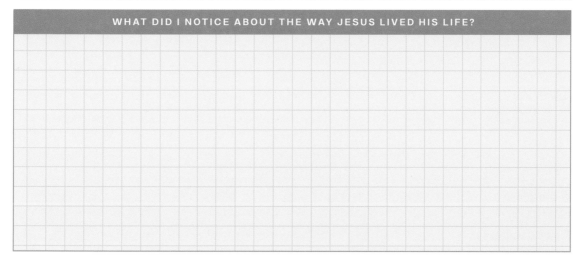

WHAT DID I NOTICE ABOUT THE WAY JESUS LIVED HIS LIFE?

Jesus's Parable of the Lost Son

He was lost and is found.

LUKE 15:24

Luke 15

The Parable of the Lost Sheep

All the tax collectors and sinners were approaching to listen to him. [2] And the Pharisees and scribes were complaining, "This man welcomes sinners and eats with them."

[3] So he told them this parable: [4] "What man among you, who has a hundred sheep and loses one of them, does not leave the ninety-nine in the open field and go after the lost one until he finds it? [5] When he has found it, he joyfully puts it on his shoulders, [6] and coming home, he calls his friends and neighbors together, saying to them, 'Rejoice with me, because I have found my lost sheep!' [7] I tell you, in the same way,

there will be more joy in heaven over one sinner who repents than over ninety-nine righteous people who don't need repentance.

The Parable of the Lost Coin

[8] "Or what woman who has ten silver coins, if she loses one coin, does not light a lamp, sweep the house, and search carefully until she finds it? [9] When she finds it, she calls her friends and neighbors together, saying, 'Rejoice with me, because I have found the silver coin I lost!' [10] I tell you, in the same way, there is joy in the presence of God's angels over one sinner who repents."

The Parable of the Lost Son

[11] He also said, "A man had two sons. [12] The younger of them said to his father, 'Father, give me the share of the estate I have coming to me.' So he distributed the assets to them. [13] Not many days later, the younger son gathered together all he had and traveled to a distant country, where he squandered his estate in foolish living. [14] After he had spent everything, a severe famine struck that country, and he had nothing. [15] Then he went to work for one of the citizens of that country, who sent him into his fields to feed pigs. [16] He longed to eat his fill from the pods that the pigs were eating, but no one would give him anything. [17] When he came to his senses, he said, 'How many of my father's hired workers have more than enough food, and here I am dying of hunger! [18] I'll get up, go to my father, and say to him, "Father, I have sinned against heaven and in your sight. [19] I'm no longer worthy to be called your son. Make me like one of your hired workers."' [20] So he got up and went to his father. But while the son was still a long way off, his father saw him and was filled with compassion. He ran, threw his arms around his neck, and kissed him. [21] The son said to him, 'Father, I have sinned against heaven and in your sight. I'm no longer worthy to be called your son.'

[22] "But the father told his servants, 'Quick! Bring out the best robe and put it on him; put a ring on his finger and sandals on his feet. [23] Then bring the fattened calf and slaughter it, and let's celebrate with a feast,

[24] because this son of mine was dead and is alive again; he was lost and is found!' So they began to celebrate.

²⁵ "Now his older son was in the field; as he came near the house, he heard music and dancing. ²⁶ So he summoned one of the servants, questioning what these things meant. ²⁷ 'Your brother is here,' he told him, 'and your father has slaughtered the fattened calf because he has him back safe and sound.'

²⁸ "Then he became angry and didn't want to go in. So his father came out and pleaded with him. ²⁹ But he replied to his father, 'Look, I have been slaving many years for you, and I have never disobeyed your orders, yet you never gave me a goat so that I could celebrate with my friends. ³⁰ But when this son of yours came, who has devoured your assets with prostitutes, you slaughtered the fattened calf for him.'

³¹ "'Son,' he said to him, 'you are always with me, and everything I have is yours.

³² But we had to celebrate and rejoice, because this brother of yours was dead and is alive again; he was lost and is found.'"

Luke 16

The Parable of the Dishonest Manager

¹ Now he said to the disciples, "There was a rich man who received an accusation that his manager was squandering his possessions. ² So he called the manager in and asked, 'What is this I hear about you? Give an account of your management, because you can no longer be my manager.'

3 "Then the manager said to himself, 'What will I do since my master is taking the management away from me? I'm not strong enough to dig; I'm ashamed to beg. 4 I know what I'll do so that when I'm removed from management, people will welcome me into their homes.'

5 "So he summoned each one of his master's debtors. 'How much do you owe my master?' he asked the first one.

6 "'A hundred measures of olive oil,' he said.

"'Take your invoice,' he told him, 'sit down quickly, and write fifty.'

7 "Next he asked another, 'How much do you owe?'

"'A hundred measures of wheat,' he said.

"'Take your invoice,' he told him, 'and write eighty.'

8 "The master praised the unrighteous manager because he had acted shrewdly. For the children of this age are more shrewd than the children of light in dealing with their own people. 9 And I tell you, make friends for yourselves by means of worldly wealth so that when it fails, they may welcome you into eternal dwellings. 10 Whoever is faithful in very little is also faithful in much, and whoever is unrighteous in very little is also unrighteous in much. 11 So if you have not been faithful with worldly wealth, who will trust you with what is genuine? 12 And if you have not been faithful with what belongs to someone else, who will give you what is your own? 13 No servant can serve two masters, since either he will hate one and love the other, or he will be devoted to one and despise the other. You cannot serve both God and money."

Kingdom Values

[14] The Pharisees, who were lovers of money, were listening to all these things and scoffing at him. [15] And he told them, "You are the ones who justify yourselves in the sight of others, but God knows your hearts. For what is highly admired by people is revolting in God's sight.

[16] "The Law and the Prophets were until John; since then, the good news of the kingdom of God has been proclaimed, and everyone is urgently invited to enter it. [17] But it is easier for heaven and earth to pass away than for one stroke of a letter in the law to drop out.

[18] "Everyone who divorces his wife and marries another woman commits adultery, and everyone who marries a woman divorced from her husband commits adultery.

The Rich Man and Lazarus

[19] "There was a rich man who would dress in purple and fine linen, feasting lavishly every day. [20] But a poor man named Lazarus, covered with sores, was lying at his gate. [21] He longed to be filled with what fell from the rich man's table, but instead the dogs would come and lick his sores. [22] One day the poor man died and was carried away by the angels to Abraham's side. The rich man also died and was buried. [23] And being in torment in Hades, he looked up and saw Abraham a long way off, with Lazarus at his side. [24] 'Father Abraham!' he called out, 'Have mercy on me and send Lazarus to dip the tip of his finger in water and cool my tongue, because I am in agony in this flame!'

²⁵ "'Son,' Abraham said, 'remember that during your life you received your good things, just as Lazarus received bad things, but now he is comforted here, while you are in agony. ²⁶ Besides all this, a great chasm has been fixed between us and you, so that those who want to pass over from here to you cannot; neither can those from there cross over to us.'

²⁷ "'Father,' he said, 'then I beg you to send him to my father's house— ²⁸ because I have five brothers—to warn them, so that they won't also come to this place of torment.'

²⁹ "But Abraham said, 'They have Moses and the prophets; they should listen to them.'

³⁰ "'No, father Abraham,' he said. 'But if someone from the dead goes to them, they will repent.'

³¹ "But he told him, 'If they don't listen to Moses and the prophets, they will not be persuaded if someone rises from the dead.'"

DATE   /   /

SUMMARIZE TODAY'S READING.

WHAT IS SOMETHING I LEARNED OR WAS REMINDED OF ABOUT JESUS?

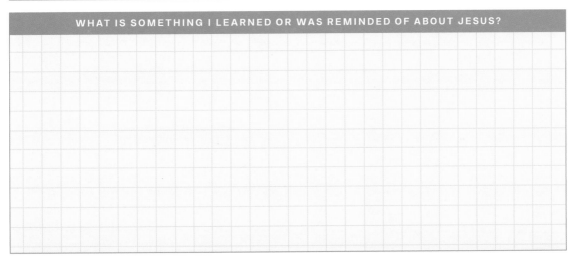

WHAT DID I NOTICE ABOUT THE WAY JESUS LIVED HIS LIFE?

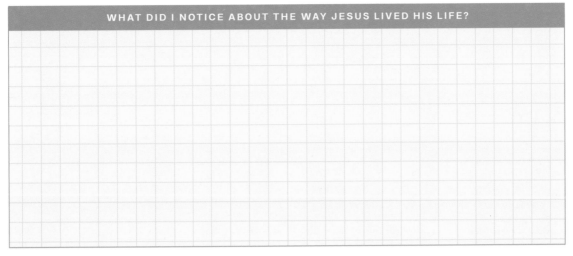

Jesus Visits Zaccheus

"For the Son of Man has come to seek and to save the lost."

LUKE 19:10

4.23.23

Luke 18:18–42

SEE MT 19:16–30; MK 10:17–30

The Rich Young Ruler

¹⁸ A ruler asked him, "Good teacher, what must I do to inherit eternal life?"

¹⁹ "Why do you call me good?" Jesus asked him. "No one is good except God alone. ²⁰ You know the commandments: Do not commit adultery; do not murder; do not steal; do not bear false witness; honor your father and mother."

²¹ "I have kept all these from my youth," he said.

²² When Jesus heard this, he told him, "You still lack one thing: Sell all you have and distribute it to the poor, and you will have treasure in heaven. Then come, follow me."

²³ After he heard this, he became extremely sad, because he was very rich.

Possessions and the Kingdom

²⁴ Seeing that he became sad, Jesus said, "How hard it is for those who have wealth to enter the kingdom of God! ²⁵ For it is easier for a camel to go through the eye of a needle than for a rich person to enter the kingdom of God."

²⁶ Those who heard this asked, "Then who can be saved?"

²⁷ He replied, "What is impossible with man is possible with God."

²⁸ Then Peter said, "Look, we have left what we had and followed you."

²⁹ So he said to them, "Truly I tell you, there is no one who has left a house, wife or brothers or sisters, parents or children because of the kingdom of God, ³⁰ who will not receive many times more at this time, and eternal life in the age to come."

The Third Prediction of His Death

[31] Then he took the Twelve aside and told them, "See, we are going up to Jerusalem. Everything that is written through the prophets about the Son of Man will be accomplished. [32] For he will be handed over to the Gentiles, and he will be mocked, insulted, spit on; [33] and after they flog him, they will kill him, and he will rise on the third day."

[34] They understood none of these things. The meaning of the saying was hidden from them, and they did not grasp what was said.

A Blind Man Receives His Sight

[35] As he approached Jericho, a blind man was sitting by the road begging. [36] Hearing a crowd passing by, he inquired what was happening. [37] "Jesus of Nazareth is passing by," they told him.

[38] So he called out, "Jesus, Son of David, have mercy on me!" [39] Then those in front told him to keep quiet, but he kept crying out all the more, "Son of David, have mercy on me!"

[40] Jesus stopped and commanded that he be brought to him. When he came closer, he asked him, [41] "What do you want me to do for you?"

"Lord," he said, "I want to see."

[42] "Receive your sight," Jesus told him. "Your faith has saved you."

Luke 19:1–28

Jesus Visits Zacchaeus

[1] He entered Jericho and was passing through. [2] There was a man named Zacchaeus who was a chief tax collector, and he was rich. [3] He was trying to see who Jesus was, but he was not able because of the crowd, since he was a short man. [4] So running ahead, he climbed up a sycamore tree to see Jesus,

SEE MT 20:29-34; MK 10:46-52

since he was about to pass that way. [5] When Jesus came to the place, he looked up and said to him, "Zacchaeus, hurry and come down because today it is necessary for me to stay at your house."

[6] So he quickly came down and welcomed him joyfully. [7] All who saw it began to complain, "He's gone to stay with a sinful man."

[8] But Zacchaeus stood there and said to the Lord, "Look, I'll give half of my possessions to the poor, Lord. And if I have extorted anything from anyone, I'll pay back four times as much."

[9] "Today salvation has come to this house," Jesus told him, "because he too is a son of Abraham. [10] For the Son of Man has come to seek and to save the lost."

The Parable of the Ten Minas

[11] As they were listening to this, he went on to tell a parable because he was near Jerusalem, and they thought the kingdom of God was going to appear right away.

[12] Therefore he said, "A nobleman traveled to a far country to receive for himself authority to be king and then to return. [13] He called ten of his servants, gave them ten minas, and told them, 'Engage in business until I come back.'

[14] "But his subjects hated him and sent a delegation after him, saying, 'We don't want this man to rule over us.'

[15] "At his return, having received the authority to be king, he summoned those servants he had given the money to, so that he could find out how much they had made in business. [16] The first came forward and said, 'Master, your mina has earned ten more minas.'

[17] "'Well done, good servant!' he told him. 'Because you have been faithful in a very small matter, have authority over ten towns.'

[18] "The second came and said, 'Master, your mina has made five minas.'

[19] "So he said to him, 'You will be over five towns.'

[20] "And another came and said, 'Master, here is your mina. I have kept it safe in a cloth [21] because I was afraid of you since you're a harsh man: you collect what you didn't deposit and reap what you didn't sow.'

[22] "He told him, 'I will condemn you by what you have said, you evil servant! If you knew I was a harsh man, collecting what I didn't deposit and reaping what I didn't sow, [23] why, then, didn't you put my money in the bank? And when I returned, I would have collected it with interest.' [24] So he said to those standing there, 'Take the mina away from him and give it to the one who has ten minas.'

[25] "But they said to him, 'Master, he has ten minas.'

[26] "'I tell you, that to everyone who has, more will be given; and from the one who does not have, even what he does have will be taken away. [27] But bring here these enemies of mine, who did not want me to rule over them, and slaughter them in my presence.'"

[28] When he had said these things, he went on ahead, going up to Jerusalem.

DATE   /   /

SUMMARIZE TODAY'S READING.

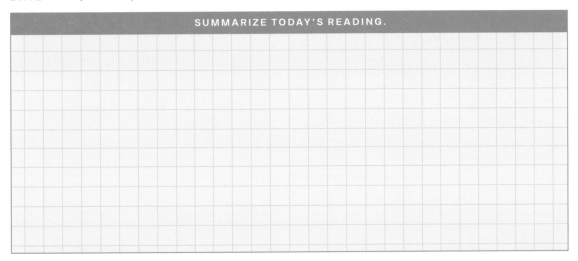

WHAT IS SOMETHING I LEARNED OR WAS REMINDED OF ABOUT JESUS?

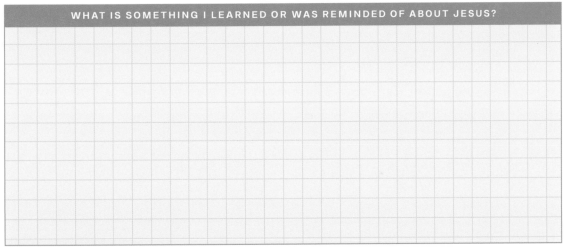

WHAT DID I NOTICE ABOUT THE WAY JESUS LIVED HIS LIFE?

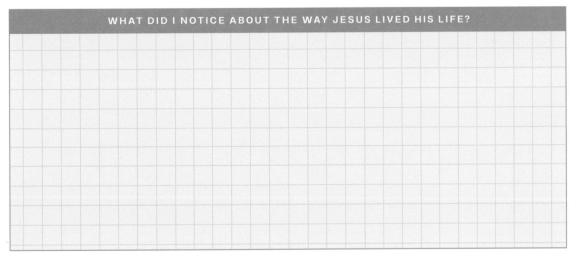

Grace Day

Take this day to catch up on your reading, pray, and rest in the presence of the Lord.

"This is my beloved
Son, with whom
I am well-pleased.
Listen to him!"

Matthew 17:5

Weekly Truth

*Scripture is God-breathed and true. When we memorize it,
we carry the good news of Jesus with us wherever we go.*

This week, as we continue to memorize Matthew 9:35–36,
we will add the first part of verse 36—Jesus's response
to the people He ministered to.

Jesus continued going around to all the towns and villages, teaching in their synagogues, preaching the good news of the kingdom, and healing every disease and every sickness. When he saw the crowds, he felt compassion for them, because they were distressed and dejected, like sheep without a shepherd.

MATTHEW 9:35–36

See tips for memorizing Scripture on page 188.

The Triumphal Entry

Blessed is he who comes in the name of the Lord!

MATTHEW 21:9

WEEK 04   DAY 22

Matthew 26:6–16

The Anointing at Bethany

SEE MK 14:3–9

6 While Jesus was in Bethany at the house of Simon the leper, 7 a woman approached him with an alabaster jar of very expensive perfume. She poured it on his head as he was reclining at the table. 8 When the disciples saw it, they were indignant. "Why this waste?" they asked. 9 "This might have been sold for a great deal and given to the poor."

10 Aware of this, Jesus said to them, "Why are you bothering this woman? She has done a noble thing for me. 11 You always have the poor with you, but you do not always have me. 12 By pouring this perfume on my body, she has prepared me for burial. 13 Truly I tell you, wherever this gospel is proclaimed in the whole world, what she has done will also be told in memory of her."

14 Then one of the Twelve, the man called Judas Iscariot, went to the chief priests 15 and said, "What are you willing to give me if I hand him over to you?" So they weighed out thirty pieces of silver for him. 16 And from that time he started looking for a good opportunity to betray him.

Matthew 21

The Triumphal Entry

[1] When they approached Jerusalem and came to Bethphage at the Mount of Olives, Jesus then sent two disciples, [2] telling them, "Go into the village ahead of you. At once you will find a donkey tied there with her colt. Untie them and bring them to me. [3] If anyone says anything to you, say that the Lord needs them, and he will send them at once."

[4] This took place so that what was spoken through the prophet might be fulfilled:

[5] Tell Daughter Zion,
"See, your King is coming to you,
gentle, and mounted on a donkey,
and on a colt,
the foal of a donkey."

[6] The disciples went and did just as Jesus directed them. [7] They brought the donkey and the colt; then they laid their clothes on them, and he sat on them. [8] A very large crowd spread their clothes on the road; others were cutting branches from the trees and spreading them on the road. [9] Then the crowds who went ahead of him and those who followed shouted:

Hosanna to the Son of David!
Blessed is he who comes in the name
of the Lord!
Hosanna in the highest heaven!

[10] When he entered Jerusalem, the whole city was in an uproar, saying, "Who is this?" [11] The crowds were saying,

"This is the prophet Jesus from Nazareth in Galilee."

Cleansing the Temple

[12] Jesus went into the temple and threw out all those buying and selling. He overturned the tables of the money changers and the chairs of those selling doves. [13] He said to them, "It is written, my house will be called a house of prayer, but you are making it a den of thieves!"

SEE MK 11:1-10

SEE MK 11:15-17

Children Praise Jesus

[14] The blind and the lame came to him in the temple, and he healed them. [15] When the chief priests and the scribes saw the wonders that he did and the children shouting in the temple, "*Hosanna* to the Son of David!" they were indignant [16] and said to him, "Do you hear what these children are saying?"

Jesus replied, "Yes, have you never read:

> You have prepared praise
> from the mouths of infants and nursing babies?"

SEE MK 11:11

[17] Then he left them, went out of the city to Bethany, and spent the night there.

The Barren Fig Tree

SEE MK 11:12–14

[18] Early in the morning, as he was returning to the city, he was hungry. [19] Seeing a lone fig tree by the road, he went up to it and found nothing on it except leaves. And he said to it, "May no fruit ever come from you again!" At once the fig tree withered.

SEE MK 11:20–33

[20] When the disciples saw it, they were amazed and said, "How did the fig tree wither so quickly?"

[21] Jesus answered them, "Truly I tell you, if you have faith and do not doubt, you will not only do what was done to the fig tree, but even if you tell this mountain, 'Be lifted up and thrown into the sea,' it will be done. [22] And if you believe, you will receive whatever you ask for in prayer."

The Authority of Jesus Challenged

[23] When he entered the temple, the chief priests and the elders of the people came to him as he was teaching and said, "By what authority are you doing these things? Who gave you this authority?"

[24] Jesus answered them, "I will also ask you one question, and if you answer it for me, then I will tell you by what authority I do these things. [25] Did John's baptism come from heaven, or was it of human origin?"

They discussed it among themselves, "If we say, 'From heaven,' he will say to us, 'Then why didn't you believe him?' ²⁶ But if we say, 'Of human origin,' we're afraid of the crowd, because everyone considers John to be a prophet." ²⁷ So they answered Jesus, "We don't know."

And he said to them, "Neither will I tell you by what authority I do these things.

The Parable of the Two Sons

²⁸ "What do you think? A man had two sons. He went to the first and said, 'My son, go work in the vineyard today.'

²⁹ "He answered, 'I don't want to,' but later he changed his mind and went. ³⁰ Then the man went to the other and said the same thing. 'I will, sir,' he answered, but he didn't go. ³¹ Which of the two did his father's will?"

They said, "The first."

Jesus said to them, "Truly I tell you, tax collectors and prostitutes are entering the kingdom of God before you. ³² For John came to you in the way of righteousness, and you didn't believe him. Tax collectors and prostitutes did believe him; but you, when you saw it, didn't even change your minds then and believe him.

The Parable of the Vineyard Owner

³³ "Listen to another parable: There was a landowner, who planted a vineyard, put a fence around it, dug a winepress in it, and built a watchtower. He leased it to tenant farmers and went away. ³⁴ When the time came to harvest fruit, he sent his servants to the farmers to collect his fruit. ³⁵ The farmers took his servants, beat one, killed another, and stoned a third. ³⁶ Again, he sent other servants, more than the first group, and they did the same to them. ³⁷ Finally, he sent his son to them. 'They will respect my son,' he said.

SEE MK 12:1–9; LK 20:9–19

[38] "But when the tenant farmers saw the son, they said to each other, 'This is the heir. Come, let's kill him and take his inheritance.' [39] So they seized him, threw him out of the vineyard, and killed him. [40] Therefore, when the owner of the vineyard comes, what will he do to those farmers?"

[41] "He will completely destroy those terrible men," they told him, "and lease his vineyard to other farmers who will give him his fruit at the harvest."

[42] Jesus said to them, "Have you never read in the Scriptures:

> The stone that the builders rejected
> has become the cornerstone.
> This is what the Lord has done
> and it is wonderful in our eyes?

[43] Therefore I tell you, the kingdom of God will be taken away from you and given to a people producing its fruit. [44] Whoever falls on this stone will be broken to pieces; but on whomever it falls, it will shatter him."

[45] When the chief priests and the Pharisees heard his parables, they knew he was speaking about them. [46] Although they were looking for a way to arrest him, they feared the crowds, because the people regarded him as a prophet.

DATE   /   /

SUMMARIZE TODAY'S READING.

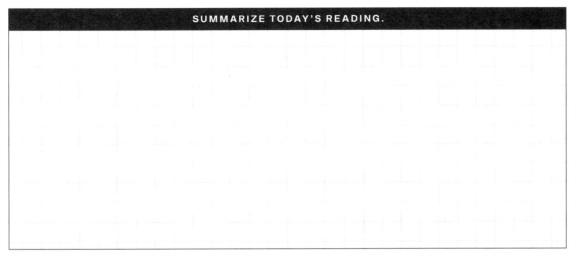

WHAT IS SOMETHING I LEARNED OR WAS REMINDED OF ABOUT JESUS?

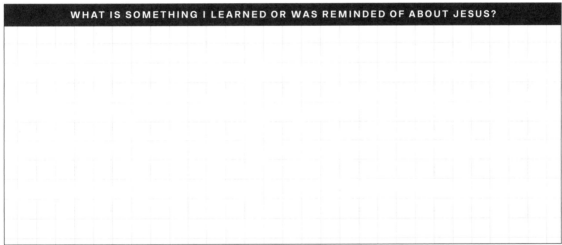

WHAT DID I NOTICE ABOUT THE WAY JESUS LIVED HIS LIFE?

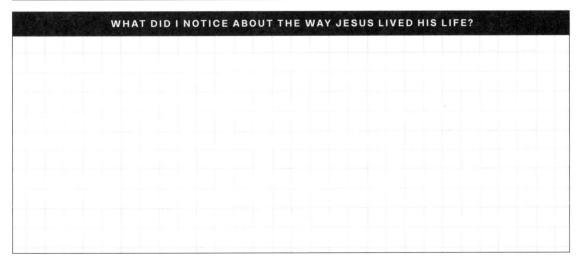

Jesus Teaches on the Primary Commands

"Love the Lord your God with all your heart, with all your soul, and with all your mind."

MATTHEW 22:37

Matthew 22

The Parable of the Wedding Banquet

Once more Jesus spoke to them in parables: [2] "The kingdom of heaven is like a king who gave a wedding banquet for his son. [3] He sent his servants to summon those invited to the banquet, but they didn't want to come. [4] Again, he sent out other servants and said, 'Tell those who are invited: See, I've prepared my dinner; my oxen and fattened cattle have been slaughtered, and everything is ready. Come to the wedding banquet.'

[5] "But they paid no attention and went away, one to his own farm, another to his business, [6] while the rest seized his servants, mistreated them, and killed them. [7] The king was enraged, and he sent out his troops, killed those murderers, and burned down their city.

[8] "Then he told his servants, 'The banquet is ready, but those who were invited were not worthy. [9] Go then to where the roads exit the city and invite everyone you find to the banquet.' [10] So those servants went out on the roads and gathered everyone they found, both evil and good. The wedding banquet was filled with guests. [11] When the king came in to see the guests, he saw a man there who was not dressed for a wedding. [12] So he said to him, 'Friend, how did you get in here without wedding clothes?' The man was speechless.

[13] "Then the king told the attendants, 'Tie him up hand and foot, and throw him into the outer darkness, where there will be weeping and gnashing of teeth.'

[14] "For many are invited, but few are chosen."

God and Caesar

[15] Then the Pharisees went and plotted how to trap him by what he said. [16] So they sent their disciples to him, along with the Herodians. "Teacher," they said, "we know that you are truthful and teach truthfully the way of God. You don't care what anyone thinks nor do you show partiality. [17] Tell us, then, what you think. Is it lawful to pay taxes to Caesar or not?"

[18] Perceiving their malicious intent, Jesus said, "Why are you testing me, hypocrites? [19] Show me the coin used for the tax." They brought him a denarius. [20] "Whose image and inscription is this?" he asked them.

[21] "Caesar's," they said to him.

Then he said to them,

"Give, then, to Caesar the things that are Caesar's, and to God the things that are God's."

[22] When they heard this, they were amazed. So they left him and went away.

SEE MK 12:13–37; LK 20:20–44

The Sadducees and the Resurrection

23 That same day some Sadducees, who say there is no resurrection, came up to him and questioned him: 24 "Teacher, Moses said, if a man dies, having no children, his brother is to marry his wife and raise up offspring for his brother. 25 Now there were seven brothers among us. The first got married and died. Having no offspring, he left his wife to his brother. 26 The same thing happened to the second also, and the third, and so on to all seven. 27 Last of all, the woman died. 28 In the resurrection, then, whose wife will she be of the seven? For they all had married her."

29 Jesus answered them, "You are mistaken, because you don't know the Scriptures or the power of God. 30 For in the resurrection they neither marry nor are given in marriage but are like angels in heaven. 31 Now concerning the resurrection of the dead, haven't you read what was spoken to you by God: 32 I am the God of Abraham and the God of Isaac and the God of Jacob? He is not the God of the dead, but of the living."

33 And when the crowds heard this, they were astonished at his teaching.

The Primary Commands

34 When the Pharisees heard that he had silenced the Sadducees, they came together. 35 And one of them, an expert in the law, asked a question to test him: 36 "Teacher, which command in the law is the greatest?"

37 He said to him, "Love the Lord your God with all your heart, with all your soul, and with all your mind. 38 This is the greatest and most important command. 39 The second is like it: Love your neighbor as yourself. 40 All the Law and the Prophets depend on these two commands."

The Question About the Messiah

41 While the Pharisees were together, Jesus questioned them, 42 "What do you think about the Messiah? Whose son is he?"

They replied, "David's."

43 He asked them, "How is it then that David, inspired by the Spirit, calls him 'Lord':

44 The Lord declared to my Lord,
'Sit at my right hand
until I put your enemies under your feet'?

45 "If David calls him 'Lord,' how, then, can he be his son?" 46 No one was able to answer him at all, and from that day no one dared to question him anymore.

DATE   /   /

SUMMARIZE TODAY'S READING.

WHAT IS SOMETHING I LEARNED OR WAS REMINDED OF ABOUT JESUS?

WHAT DID I NOTICE ABOUT THE WAY JESUS LIVED HIS LIFE?

Jesus Teaches Against Hypocrisy

—

*"Whoever exalts himself will be humbled,
and whoever humbles himself will be exalted."*

MATTHEW 23:12

Matthew 23

Religious Hypocrites Denounced

Then Jesus spoke to the crowds and to his disciples: 2 "The scribes and the Pharisees are seated in the chair of Moses. 3 Therefore do whatever they tell you, and observe it. But don't do what they do, because they don't practice what they teach. 4 They tie up heavy loads that are hard to carry and put them on people's shoulders, but they themselves aren't willing to lift a finger to move them. 5 They do everything to be seen by others: They enlarge their phylacteries and lengthen their tassels. 6 They love the place of honor at banquets, the front seats in the synagogues, 7 greetings in the marketplaces, and to be called 'Rabbi' by people.

8 "But you are not to be called 'Rabbi,' because you have one Teacher, and you are all brothers and sisters. 9 Do not call anyone on earth your father, because you have one Father, who is in heaven. 10 You are not to be called instructors either, because you have one Instructor, the Messiah. 11 The greatest among you will be your servant. 12 Whoever exalts himself will be humbled, and whoever humbles himself will be exalted.

13 "Woe to you, scribes and Pharisees, hypocrites! You shut the door of the kingdom of heaven in people's faces. For you don't go in, and you don't allow those entering to go in.

15 "Woe to you, scribes and Pharisees, hypocrites! You travel over land and sea to make one convert, and when he becomes one, you make him twice as much a child of hell as you are!

16 "Woe to you, blind guides, who say, 'Whoever takes an oath by the temple, it means nothing. But whoever takes an oath by the gold of the temple is bound by his oath.' 17 Blind fools! For which is greater, the gold or the temple that sanctified the gold? 18 Also, 'Whoever takes an oath by the altar, it means nothing; but whoever takes an oath by the gift that is on it is bound by his oath.' 19 Blind people! For which is greater, the gift or the altar that sanctifies the gift? 20 Therefore, the one who takes an oath by the altar takes an oath by it and by everything on it. 21 The one who takes an oath by the temple takes an oath by it and by him who dwells in it. 22 And the one who takes an oath by heaven takes an oath by God's throne and by him who sits on it.

23 "Woe to you, scribes and Pharisees, hypocrites! You pay a tenth of mint, dill, and cumin, and yet you have neglected the more important matters of the law—justice, mercy, and faithfulness. These things should have been done without neglecting the others. 24 Blind guides! You strain out a gnat, but gulp down a camel!

25 "Woe to you, scribes and Pharisees, hypocrites!

You clean the outside of the cup and dish, but inside they are full of greed and self-indulgence.

26 Blind Pharisee! First clean the inside of the cup, so that the outside of it may also become clean.

27 "Woe to you, scribes and Pharisees, hypocrites! You are like whitewashed tombs, which appear beautiful on the outside, but inside are full of the bones of the dead and every kind of impurity. 28 In the same way, on the outside you seem righteous to people, but inside you are full of hypocrisy and lawlessness.

29 "Woe to you, scribes and Pharisees, hypocrites! You build the tombs of the prophets and decorate the graves of the righteous, 30 and you say, 'If we had lived in the days of our ancestors, we wouldn't have taken part with them in shedding the prophets' blood.' 31 So you testify against yourselves that you are descendants of those who murdered the prophets. 32 Fill up, then, the measure of your ancestors' sins!

SEE LK 13:34–35

³³ "Snakes! Brood of vipers! How can you escape being condemned to hell? ³⁴ This is why I am sending you prophets, sages, and scribes. Some of them you will kill and crucify, and some of them you will flog in your synagogues and pursue from town to town. ³⁵ So all the righteous blood shed on the earth will be charged to you, from the blood of righteous Abel to the blood of Zechariah, son of Berechiah, whom you murdered between the sanctuary and the altar. ³⁶ Truly I tell you, all these things will come on this generation.

Jesus's Lamenting over Jerusalem

³⁷ "Jerusalem, Jerusalem, who kills the prophets and stones those who are sent to her. How often I wanted to gather your children together, as a hen gathers her chicks under her wings, but you were not willing! ³⁸ See, your house is left to you desolate. ³⁹ For I tell you, you will not see me again until you say, 'Blessed is he who comes in the name of the Lord'!"

Mark 12:38–44

Warning Against the Scribes

³⁸ He also said in his teaching, "Beware of the scribes, who want to go around in long robes and who want greetings in the marketplaces, ³⁹ the best seats in the synagogues, and the places of honor at banquets. ⁴⁰ They devour widows' houses and say long prayers just for show. These will receive harsher judgment."

The Widow's Gift

⁴¹ Sitting across from the temple treasury, he watched how the crowd dropped money into the treasury. Many rich people were putting in large sums. ⁴² Then a poor widow came and dropped in two tiny coins worth very little. ⁴³ Summoning his disciples, he said to them, "Truly I tell you, this poor widow has put more into the treasury than all the others. ⁴⁴ For they all gave out of their surplus,

but she out of her poverty has put in everything she had—all she had to live on."

DATE   /   /

WHAT IS SOMETHING I LEARNED OR WAS REMINDED OF ABOUT JESUS?

WHAT DID I NOTICE ABOUT THE WAY JESUS LIVED HIS LIFE?

How Sweet the Name of Jesus Sounds

1. How sweet the name of Je - sus sounds in a be -
2. It makes the wound - ed spir - it whole and calms the
3. Dear name— the rock on which I build, My shield and
4. Je - sus, my shep - herd, broth - er, friend, My proph - et,

liev - er's ear! It soothes his sor - rows, heals his wounds, And
trou - bled breast; 'Tis man - na to the hun - gry soul, And
hid - ing place; My nev - er - fail - ing trea - sure, filled with
priest and King. My Lord, my life, my way, my end, Ac -

drives a - way his fear, And drives a - way his fear.
to the wea - ry, rest, And to the wea - ry, rest.
bound - less stores of grace, With bound - less stores of grace!
cept the praise I bring, Ac - cept the praise I bring.

WORDS: John Newton | **MUSIC:** Thomas Hastings

The Coming of the Son of Man

—

"The Son of Man is coming at an hour you do not expect."

MATTHEW 24:44

Matthew 24

Destruction of the Temple Predicted

As Jesus left and was going out of the temple, his disciples came up and called his attention to its buildings. ² He replied to them, "Do you see all these things? Truly I tell you, not one stone will be left here on another that will not be thrown down."

Signs of the End of the Age

³ While he was sitting on the Mount of Olives, the disciples approached him privately and said, "Tell us, when will these things happen? And what is the sign of your coming and of the end of the age?"

⁴ Jesus replied to them, "Watch out that no one deceives you. ⁵ For many will come in my name, saying, 'I am the Messiah,' and they will deceive many. ⁶ You are going to hear of wars and rumors of wars. See that you are not alarmed, because these things must take place, but the end is not yet. ⁷ For nation will rise up against nation, and kingdom against kingdom. There will be famines and earthquakes in various places. ⁸ All these events are the beginning of labor pains.

SEE MK 13:1–20; LK 21:5–24

Persecutions Predicted

[9] "Then they will hand you over to be persecuted, and they will kill you. You will be hated by all nations because of my name. [10] Then many will fall away, betray one another, and hate one another. [11] Many false prophets will rise up and deceive many. [12] Because lawlessness will multiply, the love of many will grow cold. [13] But the one who endures to the end will be saved. [14] This good news of the kingdom will be proclaimed in all the world as a testimony to all nations, and then the end will come.

The Great Tribulation

[15] "So when you see the abomination of desolation, spoken of by the prophet Daniel, standing in the holy place" (let the reader understand), [16] "then those in Judea must flee to the mountains. [17] A man on the housetop must not come down to get things out of his house, [18] and a man in the field must not go back to get his coat. [19] Woe to pregnant women and nursing mothers in those days! [20] Pray that your escape may not be in winter or on a Sabbath. [21] For at that time there will be great distress, the kind that hasn't taken place from the beginning of the world until now and never will again. [22] Unless those days were cut short, no one would be saved. But those days will be cut short because of the elect.

[23] "If anyone tells you then, 'See, here is the Messiah!' or, 'Over here!' do not believe it. [24] For false messiahs and false prophets will arise and perform great signs and wonders to lead astray, if possible, even the elect. [25] Take note: I have told you in advance. [26] So if they tell you, 'See, he's in the wilderness!' don't go out; or, 'See, he's in the storerooms!' do not believe it. [27] For as the lightning comes from the east and flashes as far as the west, so will be the coming of the Son of Man. [28] Wherever the carcass is, there the vultures will gather.

SEE MK 13:21-23

The Coming of the Son of Man

[29] "Immediately after the distress of those days, the sun will be darkened, and the moon will not shed its light; the stars will fall from the sky, and the powers of the heavens will be shaken.

[30] Then the sign of the Son of Man will appear in the sky,

and then all the peoples of the earth will mourn; and they will see the Son of Man coming on the clouds of heaven with power and great glory. [31] He will send out his angels with a loud trumpet, and they will gather his elect from the four winds, from one end of the sky to the other.

The Parable of the Fig Tree

[32] "Learn this lesson from the fig tree: As soon as its branch becomes tender and sprouts leaves, you know that summer is near. [33] In the same way, when you see all these things, recognize that he is near—at the door. [34] Truly I tell you, this generation will certainly not pass away until all these things take place. [35] Heaven and earth will pass away, but my words will never pass away.

No One Knows the Day or Hour

[36] "Now concerning that day and hour no one knows—neither the angels of heaven nor the Son—except the Father alone. [37] As the days of Noah were, so the coming of the Son of Man will be. [38] For in those days before the flood they were eating and drinking, marrying and giving in marriage, until the day Noah boarded the ark. [39] They didn't know until the flood came and swept them all away. This is the way the coming of the Son of Man will be. [40] Then two men will be in the field; one will be taken and one left. [41] Two women will be grinding grain with a hand mill; one will be taken and one left. [42] Therefore be alert, since you don't know what

SEE MK 13:24-32; LK 21:25-33

SEE MK 13:33-37; LK 21:34-36

day your Lord is coming. [43] But know this: If the homeowner had known what time the thief was coming, he would have stayed alert and not let his house be broken into. [44] This is why you are also to be ready, because the Son of Man is coming at an hour you do not expect.

Faithful Service to Christ

[45] "Who then is a faithful and wise servant, whom his master has put in charge of his household, to give them food at the proper time? [46] Blessed is that servant whom the master finds doing his job when he comes. [47] Truly I tell you, he will put him in charge of all his possessions. [48] But if that wicked servant says in his heart, 'My master is delayed,' [49] and starts to beat his fellow servants, and eats and drinks with drunkards, [50] that servant's master will come on a day he does not expect him and at an hour he does not know. [51] He will cut him to pieces and assign him a place with the hypocrites, where there will be weeping and gnashing of teeth."

DATE   /   /

SUMMARIZE TODAY'S READING.

WHAT IS SOMETHING I LEARNED OR WAS REMINDED OF ABOUT JESUS?

WHAT DID I NOTICE ABOUT THE WAY JESUS LIVED HIS LIFE?

The Kingdom of Heaven

—

"Be alert, because you don't know either the day or the hour."

MATTHEW 25:13

Matthew 25

The Parable of the Ten Virgins

"At that time the kingdom of heaven will be like ten virgins who took their lamps and went out to meet the groom. ² Five of them were foolish and five were wise. ³ When the foolish took their lamps, they didn't take oil with them; ⁴ but the wise ones took oil in their flasks with their lamps. ⁵ When the groom was delayed, they all became drowsy and fell asleep.

⁶ "In the middle of the night there was a shout: 'Here's the groom! Come out to meet him.'

⁷ "Then all the virgins got up and trimmed their lamps. ⁸ The foolish ones said to the wise ones, 'Give us some of your oil, because our lamps are going out.'

⁹ "The wise ones answered, 'No, there won't be enough for us and for you. Go instead to those who sell oil, and buy some for yourselves.'

¹⁰ "When they had gone to buy some, the groom arrived, and those who were ready went in with him to the wedding banquet, and the door was shut. ¹¹ Later the rest of the virgins also came and said, 'Master, master, open up for us!'

¹² "He replied, 'Truly I tell you, I don't know you!'

¹³ "Therefore be alert, because you don't know either the day or the hour.

The Parable of the Talents

¹⁴ "For it is just like a man about to go on a journey. He called his own servants and entrusted his possessions to them. ¹⁵ To one he gave five talents, to another two talents, and to another one talent, depending on each one's ability. Then he went on a journey. Immediately ¹⁶ the man who had received five talents went, put them to work, and earned five more. ¹⁷ In the same way the man with two earned two

more. [18] But the man who had received one talent went off, dug a hole in the ground, and hid his master's money.

[19] "After a long time the master of those servants came and settled accounts with them. [20] The man who had received five talents approached, presented five more talents, and said, 'Master, you gave me five talents. See, I've earned five more talents.'

[21] "His master said to him,

'Well done, good and faithful servant!

You were faithful over a few things; I will put you in charge of many things. Share your master's joy.'

[22] "The man with two talents also approached. He said, 'Master, you gave me two talents. See, I've earned two more talents.'

[23] "His master said to him, 'Well done, good and faithful servant! You were faithful over a few things; I will put you in charge of many things.

Share your master's joy.'

[24] "The man who had received one talent also approached and said, 'Master, I know you. You're a harsh man, reaping where you haven't sown and gathering where you haven't scattered seed. [25] So I was afraid and went off and hid your talent in the ground. See, you have what is yours.'

[26] "His master replied to him, 'You evil, lazy servant! If you knew that I reap where I haven't sown and gather where I haven't scattered, [27] then you should have deposited my money with the bankers, and I would have received my money back with interest when I returned.

28 "'So take the talent from him and give it to the one who has ten talents. 29 For to everyone who has, more will be given, and he will have more than enough. But from the one who does not have, even what he has will be taken away from him. 30 And throw this good-for-nothing servant into the outer darkness, where there will be weeping and gnashing of teeth.'

The Sheep and the Goats

31 "When the Son of Man comes in his glory, and all the angels with him, then he will sit on his glorious throne. 32 All the nations will be gathered before him, and he will separate them one from another, just as a shepherd separates the sheep from the goats. 33 He will put the sheep on his right and the goats on the left. 34 Then the King will say to those on his right, 'Come, you who are blessed by my Father; inherit the kingdom prepared for you from the foundation of the world.

35 "'For I was hungry and you gave me something to eat; I was thirsty and you gave me something to drink; I was a stranger and you took me in; 36 I was naked and you clothed me; I was sick and you took care of me; I was in prison and you visited me.'

37 "Then the righteous will answer him, 'Lord, when did we see you hungry and feed you, or thirsty and give you something to drink? 38 When did we see you a stranger and take you in, or without clothes and clothe you? 39 When did we see you sick, or in prison, and visit you?'

40 "And the King will answer them, 'Truly I tell you, whatever you did for one of the least of these brothers and sisters of mine, you did for me.'

[41] "Then he will also say to those on the left, 'Depart from me, you who are cursed, into the eternal fire prepared for the devil and his angels! [42] For I was hungry and you gave me nothing to eat; I was thirsty and you gave me nothing to drink; [43] I was a stranger and you didn't take me in; I was naked and you didn't clothe me, sick and in prison and you didn't take care of me.'

[44] "Then they too will answer, 'Lord, when did we see you hungry, or thirsty, or a stranger, or without clothes, or sick, or in prison, and not help you?'

[45] "Then he will answer them, 'Truly I tell you, whatever you did not do for one of the least of these, you did not do for me.'

[46] "And they will go away into eternal punishment, but the righteous into eternal life."

DATE   /   /

SUMMARIZE TODAY'S READING.

WHAT IS SOMETHING I LEARNED OR WAS REMINDED OF ABOUT JESUS?

WHAT DID I NOTICE ABOUT THE WAY JESUS LIVED HIS LIFE?

Grace Day

Take this day to catch up on your reading, pray, and rest in the presence of the Lord.

Jesus answered them,
"Truly I tell you,
if you have faith and
do not doubt, you will
not only do what was
done to the fig tree,
but even if you tell this
mountain, 'Be lifted up
and thrown into the sea,'
it will be done."

Matthew 21:21

Weekly Truth

Scripture is God-breathed and true. When we memorize it,
we carry the good news of Jesus with us wherever we go.

This week we will finish our memorization of our key passage with the final section, which further highlights Jesus's compassion for the people He ministered to.

Jesus continued going around
to all the towns and villages,
teaching in their synagogues,
preaching the good news of the
kingdom, and healing every
disease and every sickness.
When he saw the crowds,
he felt compassion for them,
because they were distressed
and dejected, like sheep
without a shepherd.

MATTHEW 9:35–36

See tips for memorizing Scripture on page 188.

Jesus's Last Supper

—

And he took bread, gave thanks, broke it, gave it to them, and said,
"This is my body, which is given for you."

LUKE 22:19

Luke 22:1–38

The Plot to Kill Jesus

SEE MT 26:3–5; MK 14:1–2

The Festival of Unleavened Bread, which is called Passover, was approaching. [2] The chief priests and the scribes were looking for a way to put him to death, because they were afraid of the people.

SEE MT 26:14–16; MK 14:10–11

[3] Then Satan entered Judas, called Iscariot, who was numbered among the Twelve. [4] He went away and discussed with the chief priests and temple police how he could hand him over to them. [5] They were glad and agreed to give him silver. [6] So he accepted the offer and started looking for a good opportunity to betray him to them when the crowd was not present.

Preparation for Passover

SEE MT 26:17–20; MK 14:12–17

[7] Then the Day of Unleavened Bread came when the Passover lamb had to be sacrificed. [8] Jesus sent Peter and John, saying, "Go and make preparations for us to eat the Passover."

[9] "Where do you want us to prepare it?" they asked him.

[10] "Listen," he said to them, "when you've entered the city, a man carrying a water jug will meet you. Follow him into the house he enters. [11] Tell the owner of the house, 'The Teacher asks you, "Where is the guest room where I can eat the Passover with my disciples?"' [12] Then he will show you a large, furnished room upstairs. Make the preparations there."

[13] So they went and found it just as he had told them, and they prepared the Passover.

The First Lord's Supper

[14] When the hour came, he reclined at the table, and the apostles with him. [15] Then he said to them, "I have fervently desired to eat this Passover with you before I suffer. [16] For I tell you, I will not eat it again until it is fulfilled in the kingdom of God." [17] Then he took a cup, and after giving thanks, he said, "Take this and share it among yourselves. [18] For I tell you, from now on I will not drink of the fruit of the vine until the kingdom of God comes."

[19] And he took bread, gave thanks, broke it, gave it to them, and said, "This is my body, which is given for you.

Do this in remembrance of me."

SEE MT 26:21–25; MK 14:18–21

[20] In the same way he also took the cup after supper and said, "This cup is the new covenant in my blood, which is poured out for you. [21] But look, the hand of the one betraying me is at the table with me. [22] For the Son of Man will go away as it has been determined, but woe to that man by whom he is betrayed!"

[23] So they began to argue among themselves which of them it could be who was going to do it.

The Dispute over Greatness

[24] Then a dispute also arose among them about who should be considered the greatest. [25] But he said to them, "The kings of the Gentiles lord it over them, and those who have authority over them have themselves called 'Benefactors.' [26] It is not to be like that among you. On the contrary, whoever is greatest among you should become like the youngest, and whoever leads, like the one serving. [27] For who is greater, the one at the table or the one serving? Isn't it the one at the table? But I am among you as the one who serves. [28] You are those who stood by me in my trials. [29] I bestow on you a kingdom, just as my Father bestowed one on me, [30] so that you may eat and drink at my table in my kingdom. And you will sit on thrones judging the twelve tribes of Israel.

Peter's Denial Predicted

SEE MT 26:31–35; MK 14:27–31

[31] "Simon, Simon, look out. Satan has asked to sift you like wheat. [32] But I have prayed for you that your faith may not fail. And you, when you have turned back, strengthen your brothers."

[33] "Lord," he told him, "I'm ready to go with you both to prison and to death."

[34] "I tell you, Peter," he said, "the rooster will not crow today until you deny three times that you know me."

Be Ready for Trouble

[35] He also said to them, "When I sent you out without money-bag, traveling bag, or sandals, did you lack anything?"

"Not a thing," they said.

[36] Then he said to them, "But now, whoever has a money-bag should take it, and also a traveling bag. And whoever doesn't have a sword should sell his robe and buy one. [37] For I tell you, what is written must be fulfilled in me: And he was counted among the lawless. Yes, what is written about me is coming to its fulfillment."

[38] "Lord," they said, "look, here are two swords."

"That is enough!" he told them.

DATE   /   /

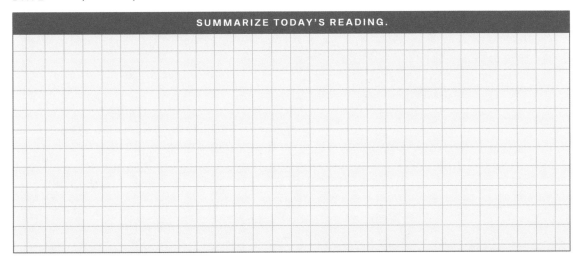

SUMMARIZE TODAY'S READING.

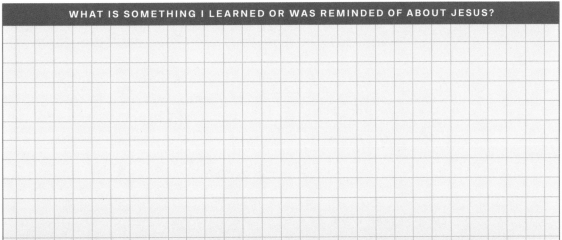

WHAT IS SOMETHING I LEARNED OR WAS REMINDED OF ABOUT JESUS?

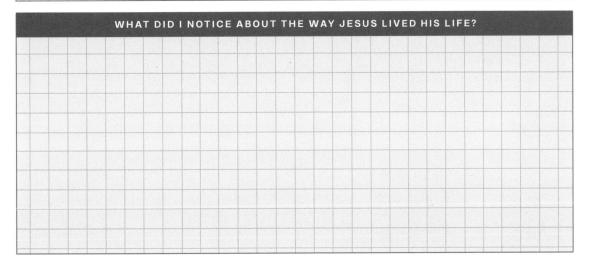

WHAT DID I NOTICE ABOUT THE WAY JESUS LIVED HIS LIFE?

Jesus
Faces Trials

I find no grounds for charging this man.

LUKE 23:4

WEEK 05   **DAY 30**

Luke 22:39–65

SEE MT 26:36-55; MK 14:32-52

The Prayer in the Garden

³⁹ He went out and made his way as usual to the Mount of Olives, and the disciples followed him. ⁴⁰ When he reached the place, he told them, "Pray that you may not fall into temptation." ⁴¹ Then he withdrew from them about a stone's throw, knelt down, and began to pray, ⁴² "Father, if you are willing, take this cup away from me—nevertheless, not my will, but yours, be done."

⁴³ Then an angel from heaven appeared to him, strengthening him. ⁴⁴ Being in anguish, he prayed more fervently, and his sweat became like drops of blood falling to the ground. ⁴⁵ When he got up from prayer and came to the disciples, he found them sleeping, exhausted from their grief. ⁴⁶ "Why are you sleeping?" he asked them. "Get up and pray, so that you won't fall into temptation."

Judas's Betrayal of Jesus

⁴⁷ While he was still speaking, suddenly a mob came, and one of the Twelve named Judas was leading them. He came near Jesus to kiss him, ⁴⁸ but Jesus said to him, "Judas, are you betraying the Son of Man with a kiss?"

⁴⁹ When those around him saw what was going to happen, they asked, "Lord, should we strike with the sword?" ⁵⁰ Then one of them struck the high priest's servant and cut off his right ear.

⁵¹ But Jesus responded, "No more of this!" And touching his ear, he healed him. ⁵² Then Jesus said to the chief priests, temple police, and the elders who had come for him, "Have you come out with swords and clubs as if I were a criminal? ⁵³ Every day while I was with you in the temple, you never laid a hand on me. But this is your hour—and the dominion of darkness."

Peter Denies His Lord

⁵⁴ They seized him, led him away, and brought him into the high priest's house. Meanwhile Peter was following at a distance. ⁵⁵ They lit a fire in the middle of the courtyard and sat down together, and Peter sat among them. ⁵⁶ When a servant saw him sitting in the light, and looked closely at him, she said, "This man was with him too."

⁵⁷ But he denied it: "Woman, I don't know him."

⁵⁸ After a little while, someone else saw him and said, "You're one of them too."

"Man, I am not!" Peter said.

⁵⁹ About an hour later, another kept insisting, "This man was certainly with him, since he's also a Galilean."

⁶⁰ But Peter said, "Man, I don't know what you're talking about!" Immediately, while he was still speaking, a rooster crowed. ⁶¹ Then the Lord turned and looked at Peter. So Peter remembered the word of the Lord, how he had said to him, "Before the rooster crows today, you will deny me three times." ⁶² And he went outside and wept bitterly.

SEE MT 26:69–75; MK 14:66–72

Jesus Mocked and Beaten

[63] The men who were holding Jesus started mocking and beating him. [64] After blindfolding him, they kept asking, "Prophesy! Who was it that hit you?" [65] And they were saying many other blasphemous things to him.

Mark 14:53–65

Jesus Faces the Sanhedrin

[53] They led Jesus away to the high priest, and all the chief priests, the elders, and the scribes assembled. [54] Peter followed him at a distance, right into the high priest's courtyard. He was sitting with the servants, warming himself by the fire.

[55] The chief priests and the whole Sanhedrin were looking for testimony against Jesus to put him to death, but they could not find any. [56] For many were giving false testimony against him, and the testimonies did not agree. [57] Some stood up and gave false testimony against him, stating, [58] "We heard him say, 'I will destroy this temple made with human hands, and in three days I will build another not made by hands.'" [59] Yet their testimony did not agree even on this.

[60] Then the high priest stood up before them all and questioned Jesus, "Don't you have an answer to what these men are testifying against you?" [61] But he kept silent and did not answer. Again the high priest questioned him, "Are you the Messiah, the Son of the Blessed One?"

[62] "I am," said Jesus, "and you will see the Son of Man seated at the right hand of Power and coming with the clouds of heaven."

⁶³ Then the high priest tore his robes and said, "Why do we still need witnesses? ⁶⁴ You have heard the blasphemy. What is your decision?" They all condemned him as deserving death.

⁶⁵ Then some began to spit on him, to blindfold him, and to beat him, saying, "Prophesy!" The temple servants also took him and slapped him.

Luke 22:66–71

Jesus Faces the Sanhedrin

⁶⁶ When daylight came, the elders of the people, both the chief priests and the scribes, convened and brought him before their Sanhedrin. ⁶⁷ They said, "If you are the Messiah, tell us."

But he said to them, "If I do tell you, you will not believe. ⁶⁸ And if I ask you, you will not answer. ⁶⁹ But from now on, the Son of Man will be seated at the right hand of the power of God."

⁷⁰ They all asked, "Are you, then, the Son of God?"

And he said to them, "You say that I am."

⁷¹ "Why do we need any more testimony," they said, "since we've heard it ourselves from his mouth?"

Luke 23:1–12

Jesus Faces Pilate

¹ Then their whole assembly rose up and brought him before Pilate. ² They began to accuse him, saying, "We found this man misleading our nation, opposing payment of taxes to Caesar, and saying that he himself is the Messiah, a king."

SEE MT 27:2, 11–14; MK 15:1–5

[3] So Pilate asked him, "Are you the king of the Jews?"

He answered him, "You say so."

[4] Pilate then told the chief priests and the crowds, "I find no grounds for charging this man."

[5] But they kept insisting, "He stirs up the people, teaching throughout all Judea, from Galilee where he started even to here."

Jesus Faces Herod Antipas

[6] When Pilate heard this, he asked if the man was a Galilean. [7] Finding that he was under Herod's jurisdiction, he sent him to Herod, who was also in Jerusalem during those days. [8] Herod was very glad to see Jesus; for a long time he had wanted to see him because he had heard about him and was hoping to see some miracle performed by him. [9] So he kept asking him questions,

but Jesus did not answer him.

[10] The chief priests and the scribes stood by, vehemently accusing him. [11] Then Herod, with his soldiers, treated him with contempt, mocked him, dressed him in bright clothing, and sent him back to Pilate. [12] That very day Herod and Pilate became friends. Previously, they had been enemies.

DATE   /   /

SUMMARIZE TODAY'S READING.

WHAT IS SOMETHING I LEARNED OR WAS REMINDED OF ABOUT JESUS?

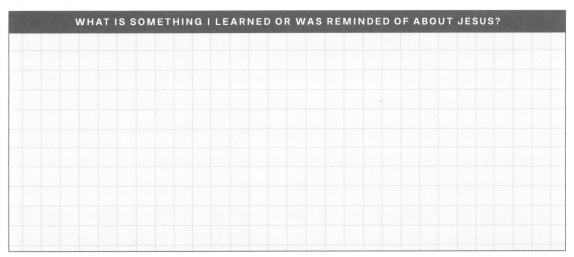

WHAT DID I NOTICE ABOUT THE WAY JESUS LIVED HIS LIFE?

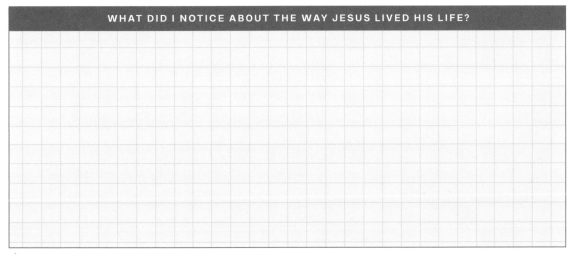

Jesus
Is Crucified

———

"Father, forgive them, because they do not know what they are doing."

LUKE 23:34

Luke 23:13–25

SEE MT 27:15–25; MK 15:6–15

Jesus or Barabbas

13 Pilate called together the chief priests, the leaders, and the people, 14 and said to them, "You have brought me this man as one who misleads the people. But in fact, after examining him in your presence, I have found no grounds to charge this man with those things you accuse him of. 15 Neither has Herod, because he sent him back to us. Clearly, he has done nothing to deserve death. 16 Therefore, I will have him whipped and then release him."

18 Then they all cried out together, "Take this man away! Release Barabbas to us!" 19 (He had been thrown into prison for a rebellion that had taken place in the city, and for murder.)

20 Wanting to release Jesus, Pilate addressed them again, 21 but they kept shouting, "Crucify! Crucify him!"

22 A third time he said to them, "Why? What has this man done wrong? I have found in him no grounds for the death penalty. Therefore, I will have him whipped and then release him."

23 But they kept up the pressure, demanding with loud voices that he be crucified, and their voices won out. 24 So Pilate decided to grant their demand 25 and released the one they were asking for, who had been thrown into prison for rebellion and murder. But he handed Jesus over to their will.

Mark 15:16–20

SEE MT 27:27–31

Mocked by the Military

16 The soldiers led him away into the palace (that is, the governor's residence) and called the whole company together. 17 They dressed him in a purple robe, twisted together a crown of thorns, and put it on him. 18 And they began to salute him, "Hail, king of the Jews!" 19 They were hitting him on the head with a stick and spitting on him. Getting down on their knees, they were paying him homage. 20 After they had mocked him, they stripped him of the purple robe and put his clothes on him.

Crucified Between Two Criminals

They led him out to crucify him.

Luke 23:26–43

The Way to the Cross

SEE MT 27:32–44; MK 15:20–32

26 As they led him away, they seized Simon, a Cyrenian, who was coming in from the country, and laid the cross on him to carry behind Jesus. 27 A large crowd of people followed him, including women who were mourning and lamenting him. 28 But turning to them, Jesus said, "Daughters of Jerusalem, do not weep for me, but weep for yourselves and your children. 29 Look, the days are coming when they will say, 'Blessed are the women without children, the wombs that never bore, and the breasts that never nursed!' 30 Then they will begin to say to the mountains, 'Fall on us!' and to the hills, 'Cover us!' 31 For if they do these things when the wood is green, what will happen when it is dry?"

Crucified Between Two Criminals

32 Two others—criminals—were also led away to be executed with him. 33 When they arrived at the place called The Skull, they crucified him there, along with the criminals, one on the right and one on the left. 34 Then Jesus said, "Father, forgive them, because they do not know what they are doing." And they divided his clothes and cast lots.

35 The people stood watching, and even the leaders were scoffing: "He saved others; let him save himself if this is God's Messiah, the Chosen One!" 36 The soldiers also mocked him. They came offering him sour wine 37 and said, "If you are the king of the Jews, save yourself!"

38 An inscription was above him:

THIS IS THE KING OF THE JEWS.

39 Then one of the criminals hanging there began to yell insults at him: "Aren't you the Messiah? Save yourself and us!"

40 But the other answered, rebuking him: "Don't you even fear God, since you are undergoing the same punishment? 41 We are punished justly, because we're getting back what we deserve for the things we did, but this man has done nothing wrong." 42 Then he said, "Jesus, remember me when you come into your kingdom."

43 And he said to him,

"Truly I tell you, today you will be with me in paradise."

DATE   /   /

SUMMARIZE TODAY'S READING.

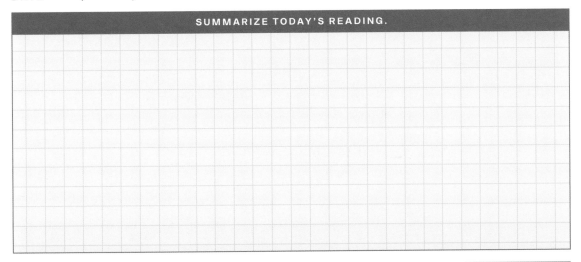

WHAT IS SOMETHING I LEARNED OR WAS REMINDED OF ABOUT JESUS?

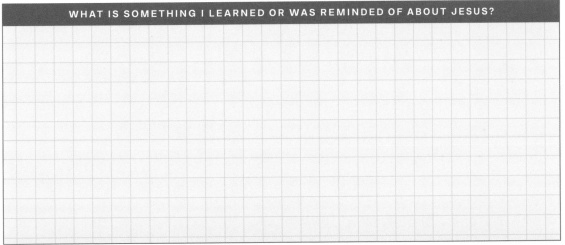

WHAT DID I NOTICE ABOUT THE WAY JESUS LIVED HIS LIFE?

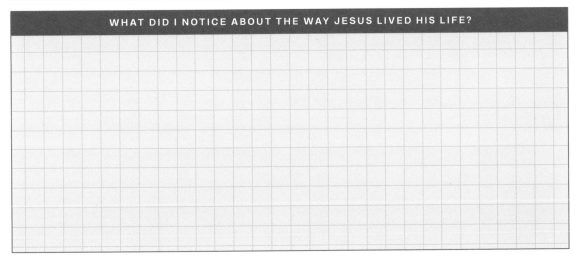

Jesus's Death and Burial

Truly this man was the Son of God!

MATTHEW 27:54

Luke 23:44–49

The Death of Jesus

⁴⁴ It was now about noon, and darkness came over the whole land until three, ⁴⁵ because the sun's light failed. The curtain of the sanctuary was split down the middle. ⁴⁶ And Jesus called out with a loud voice,

"Father, into your hands I entrust my spirit."

Saying this, he breathed his last.

⁴⁷ When the centurion saw what happened, he began to glorify God, saying, "This man really was righteous!" ⁴⁸ All the crowds that had gathered for this spectacle, when they saw what had taken place, went home, striking their chests. ⁴⁹ But all who knew him, including the women who had followed him from Galilee, stood at a distance, watching these things.

Matthew 27:45–56

The Death of Jesus

⁴⁵ From noon until three in the afternoon, darkness came over the whole land. ⁴⁶ About three in the afternoon Jesus cried out with a loud voice, *"Elí, Elí, lemá sabachtháni?"* that is,

"My God, my God, why have you abandoned me?"

⁴⁷ When some of those standing there heard this, they said, "He's calling for Elijah."

[48] Immediately one of them ran and got a sponge, filled it with sour wine, put it on a stick, and offered him a drink. [49] But the rest said, "Let's see if Elijah comes to save him."

[50] But Jesus cried out again with a loud voice and gave up his spirit. [51] Suddenly,

the curtain of the sanctuary was torn in two from top to bottom, the earth quaked, and the rocks were split. [52] The tombs were also opened and many bodies of the saints who had fallen asleep were raised.

[53] And they came out of the tombs after his resurrection, entered the holy city, and appeared to many.

[54] When the centurion and those with him, who were keeping watch over Jesus, saw the earthquake and the things that had happened, they were terrified and said, "Truly this man was the Son of God!"

[55] Many women who had followed Jesus from Galilee and looked after him were there, watching from a distance. [56] Among them were Mary Magdalene, Mary the mother of James and Joseph, and the mother of Zebedee's sons.

Luke 23:50–56

The Burial of Jesus

[50] There was a good and righteous man named Joseph, a member of the Sanhedrin, [51] who had not agreed with their plan and action. He was from Arimathea, a Judean town, and was looking forward to the kingdom of God. [52] He approached Pilate and asked for Jesus's body. [53] Taking it down, he wrapped it in fine linen and placed it in a tomb cut into the rock, where no one had ever been placed. [54] It was the preparation day, and the Sabbath was about to begin. [55] The women who had come with him from Galilee followed along and observed the tomb and how his body was placed. [56] Then they returned and prepared spices and perfumes. And they rested on the Sabbath according to the commandment.

DATE   /   /

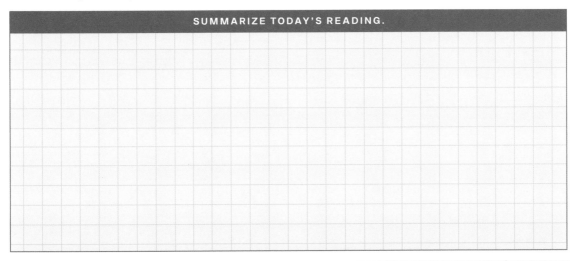

SUMMARIZE TODAY'S READING.

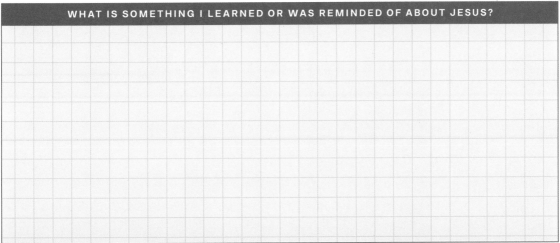

WHAT IS SOMETHING I LEARNED OR WAS REMINDED OF ABOUT JESUS?

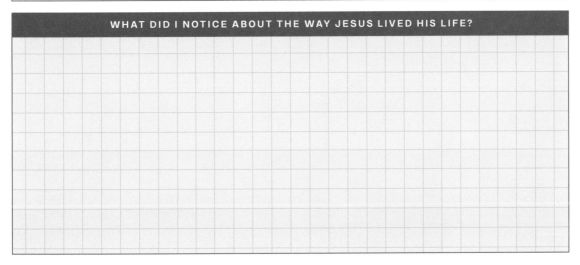

WHAT DID I NOTICE ABOUT THE WAY JESUS LIVED HIS LIFE?

Jesus Rises
from the Grave

———

The Lord has truly been raised…

LUKE 24:34

Luke 24

Resurrection Morning

[1] On the first day of the week, very early in the morning, they came to the tomb, bringing the spices they had prepared. [2] They found the stone rolled away from the tomb. [3] They went in but did not find the body of the Lord Jesus. [4] While they were perplexed about this, suddenly two men stood by them in dazzling clothes. [5] So the women were terrified and bowed down to the ground.

"Why are you looking for the living among the dead?" asked the men. [6] "He is not here, but he has risen! Remember how he spoke to you when he was still in Galilee, [7] saying, 'It is necessary that the Son of Man be betrayed into the hands of sinful men, be crucified, and rise on the third day'?" [8] And they remembered his words.

[9] Returning from the tomb, they reported all these things to the Eleven and to all the rest. [10] Mary Magdalene, Joanna, Mary the mother of James, and the other women with them were telling the apostles these things. [11] But these words seemed like nonsense to them, and they did not believe the women. [12] Peter, however, got up and ran to the tomb. When he stooped to look in, he saw only the linen cloths. So he went away, amazed at what had happened.

The Emmaus Disciples

[13] Now that same day two of them were on their way to a village called Emmaus, which was about seven miles from Jerusalem. [14] Together they were discussing everything that had taken place. [15] And while they were discussing and arguing, Jesus himself came near and began to walk along with them. [16] But they were prevented from recognizing

SEE MT 28:1–10; MK 16:1–8

him. [17] Then he asked them, "What is this dispute that you're having with each other as you are walking?" And they stopped walking and looked discouraged.

[18] The one named Cleopas answered him, "Are you the only visitor in Jerusalem who doesn't know the things that happened there in these days?"

[19] "What things?" he asked them.

So they said to him, "The things concerning Jesus of Nazareth, who was a prophet powerful in action and speech before God and all the people, [20] and how our chief priests and leaders handed him over to be sentenced to death, and they crucified him. [21] But we were hoping that he was the one who was about to redeem Israel. Besides all this, it's the third day since these things happened. [22] Moreover, some women from our group astounded us. They arrived early at the tomb, [23] and when they didn't find his body, they came and reported that they had seen a vision of angels who said he was alive. [24] Some of those who were with us went to the tomb and found it just as the women had said, but they didn't see him."

[25] He said to them, "How foolish you are, and how slow to believe all that the prophets have spoken! [26] Wasn't it necessary for the Messiah to suffer these things and enter into his glory?" [27] Then beginning with Moses and all the Prophets, he interpreted for them the things concerning himself in all the Scriptures.

²⁸ They came near the village where they were going, and he gave the impression that he was going farther. ²⁹ But they urged him, "Stay with us, because it's almost evening, and now the day is almost over." So he went in to stay with them.

³⁰ It was as he reclined at the table with them that he took the bread, blessed and broke it, and gave it to them. ³¹ Then their eyes were opened, and they recognized him, but he disappeared from their sight. ³² They said to each other, "Weren't our hearts burning within us while he was talking with us on the road and explaining the Scriptures to us?" ³³ That very hour they got up and returned to Jerusalem. They found the Eleven and those with them gathered together, ³⁴ who said, "The Lord has truly been raised and has appeared to Simon!" ³⁵ Then they began to describe what had happened on the road and how he was made known to them in the breaking of the bread.

The Reality of the Risen Jesus

³⁶ As they were saying these things, he himself stood in their midst. He said to them, "Peace to you!" ³⁷ But they were startled and terrified and thought they were seeing a ghost. ³⁸ "Why are you troubled?" he asked them. "And why do doubts arise in your hearts?

³⁹ Look at my hands and my feet, that it is I myself! Touch me and see,

because a ghost does not have flesh and bones as you can see I have." ⁴⁰ Having said this, he showed them his hands and feet. ⁴¹ But while they still were amazed and in disbelief because of their joy, he asked them, "Do you have anything here to eat?" ⁴² So they gave him a piece of a broiled fish, ⁴³ and he took it and ate in their presence.

⁴⁴ He told them, "These are my words that I spoke to you while I was still with you—that everything written about me in the Law of Moses, the Prophets, and the Psalms must be fulfilled."

⁴⁵ Then he opened their minds to understand the Scriptures.

⁴⁶ He also said to them, "This is what is written: The Messiah will suffer and rise from the dead the third day, ⁴⁷ and repentance for forgiveness of sins will be proclaimed in his name to all the nations, beginning at Jerusalem. ⁴⁸ You are witnesses of these things. ⁴⁹ And look, I am sending you what my Father promised. As for you, stay in the city until you are empowered from on high."

The Ascension of Jesus

⁵⁰ Then he led them out to the vicinity of Bethany, and lifting up his hands he blessed them. ⁵¹ And while he was blessing them, he left them and was carried up into heaven. ⁵² After worshiping him, they returned to Jerusalem with great joy. ⁵³ And they were continually in the temple praising God.

DATE   /   /

SUMMARIZE TODAY'S READING.

WHAT IS SOMETHING I LEARNED OR WAS REMINDED OF ABOUT JESUS?

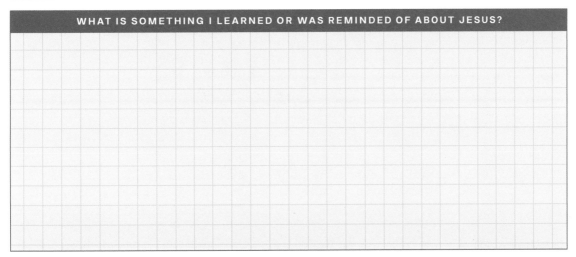

WHAT DID I NOTICE ABOUT THE WAY JESUS LIVED HIS LIFE?

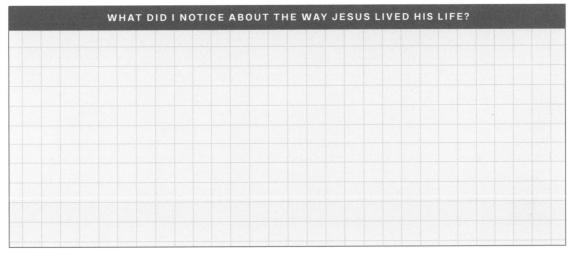

Descriptions of Jesus in Revelation

—

In the Gospel accounts, Jesus's nature is revealed: He is both fully human and fully God. Yet many people who encountered Him on earth recognized only His humanity as He walked, talked, and lived as a man. The picture of Jesus in Revelation is one of unimaginable glory and splendor, emphasizing His divinity. On the following pages you will find a collection of descriptions of Jesus in the book of Revelation, with references to where similar descriptions appear elsewhere in the Bible.

He is the One who is,
and was, and is to come.

RV 1:4, 8; 4:8; 11:17; 16:5

He is the faithful witness.

RV 1:5; 3:14   SEE PS 89:37

He is the Firstborn from the dead.

RV 1:5   SEE AC 26:23; COL 1:18

He is the ruler of the
kings of the earth.

RV 1:5   SEE PS 89:27

He is the Alpha and Omega.

RV 1:8; 21:6; 22:13

His voice is loud like a trumpet.

RV 1:10

He is the Son of Man.

RV 1:12–13; 14:14   SEE DN 7:13; MT 9:6; 10:23; 11:19

He is dressed in a robe
with a golden sash.

RV 1:13   SEE DN 10:5

His hair is white as wool and snow.

RV 1:14   SEE DN 7:9

His eyes are like a fiery flame.

RV 1:14; 2:18; 19:12   SEE DN 10:6

His feet are like fine bronze.

RV 1:15; 2:18   SEE DN 10:6

His voice is like the
sound of cascading waters.

RV 1:15   SEE EZK 1:24; 43:2

He holds seven stars
in His right hand.

RV 1:16; 2:1; 3:1

He has a sharp double-edged
sword coming from His mouth.

RV 1:16; 2:16; 19:15

His face shines like
the sun at full strength.

RV 1:16   SEE MT 17:2

He is the First and the Last.

RV 1:17; 2:8; 22:13   SEE IS 41:4; 44:6; 48:12

He is the living One.

RV 1:18   SEE MT 16:16

He is alive forever and ever.

RV 1:18   SEE RM 6:9

He holds the keys of death and Hades.

RV 1:18   SEE MT 16:18–19

He has the key of David.

RV 3:7   SEE IS 22:22

He is the Amen.

RV 3:14

He is the originator of God's creation.

RV 3:14   SEE JN 1:3

He is the Lion from
the tribe of Judah.

RV 5:5   SEE GN 49:9

He is the Root of David.

RV 5:5; 22:16   SEE IS 11:10; RM 15:12

He is like a slaughtered lamb
with seven horns and seven eyes.

RV 5:6

He is the Lamb.

☐ RV 7:17; 14:1; 17:14; 21:22   SEE JN 1:29, 36; 1PT 1:19

He shepherds His people.

☐ RV 7:17   SEE PS 23:1; JN 10:11–18

He rules with an iron rod.

☐ RV 12:5; 19:15   SEE PS 2:9

He is seated on a cloud, with a
golden crown and a sharp sickle.

☐ RV 14:14   SEE DN 7:13; LK 21:27

He tramples the winepress
of the fierce anger of God.

☐ RV 14:15–20; 19:15   SEE IS 63:3

He is Lord of lords and King of kings.

☐ RV 17:14; 19:16   SEE DT 10:17; PS 136:3; DN 2:47; 1TM 6:15

He has many crowns on His head.

☐ RV 19:12

He has a name no one
knows except Himself.

☐ RV 19:12

He wears a robe dipped in blood.

☐ RV 19:13   SEE IS 63:1–3

He is the Word of God.

☐ RV 19:13   SEE JN 1:1; HEB 4:12

He is the beginning and the end.

☐ RV 21:6; 22:13

He is the temple in the new Jerusalem.

☐ RV 21:22

He is the lamp of the new Jerusalem.

☐ RV 21:23   SEE IS 24:23; 60:19–20

He is the bright morning star.

☐ RV 22:16   SEE NM 24:17

Grace Day

Take this day to catch up on your reading,
pray, and rest in the presence of the Lord.

"But from now
on, the Son of
Man will be
seated at the
right hand of the
power of God."

Luke 22:69

Power

Weekly Truth

Scripture is God-breathed and true. When we memorize it,
we carry the good news of Jesus with us wherever we go.

For this reading plan, we worked to memorize Matthew 9:35–36.
Spend some time today reviewing the full passage. Keep this passage in
mind as you continue to grow in your understanding of Jesus's life and
ministry on earth, remembering His compassion, power, and authority.

Jesus continued going around
to all the towns and villages,
teaching in their synagogues,
preaching the good news of the
kingdom, and healing every
disease and every sickness.
When he saw the crowds,
he felt compassion for them,
because they were distressed
and dejected, like sheep
without a shepherd.

MATTHEW 9:35–36

See tips for memorizing Scripture on page 188.

healing all

Benediction

You know the events that
took place throughout all
Judea, beginning from
Galilee after the baptism
that John preached:
how God anointed
Jesus of Nazareth with
the Holy Spirit and with
power, and how he went
about doing good and
healing all who were under
the tyranny of the devil,
because God was with him.

———

ACTS 10:37–38

Tips for Memorizing Scripture

At She Reads Truth, we believe Scripture memorization is an important discipline in your walk with God. Committing God's Truth to memory means He can minister to us—and we can minister to others—through His Word no matter where we are. As you approach the Weekly Truth passage in this book, try these memorization tips to see which techniques work best for you!

STUDY IT

Study the passage in its biblical context and ask yourself a few questions before you begin to memorize it: What does this passage say? What does it mean? How would I say this in my own words? What does it teach me about God? Understanding what the passage means helps you know why it is important to carry it with you wherever you go.

Break the passage into smaller sections, memorizing a phrase at a time.

PRAY IT

Use the passage you are memorizing as a prompt for prayer.

WRITE IT

Dedicate a notebook to Scripture memorization and write the passage over and over again.

Diagram the passage after you write it out. Place a square around the verbs, underline the nouns, and circle any adjectives or adverbs. Say the passage aloud several times, emphasizing the verbs as you repeat it. Then do the same thing again with the nouns, then the adjectives and adverbs.

Write out the first letter of each word in the passage somewhere you can reference it throughout the week as you work on your memorization.

Use a whiteboard to write out the passage. Erase a few words at a time as you continue to repeat it aloud. Keep erasing parts of the passage until you have it all committed to memory.

CREATE

If you can, make up a tune for the passage to sing as you go about your day, or try singing it to the tune of a favorite song.

Sketch the passage, visualizing what each phrase would look like in the form of a picture. Or, try using calligraphy or altering the style of your handwriting as you write it out.

Use hand signals or signs to come up with associations for each word or phrase and repeat the movements as you practice.

SAY IT

Repeat the passage out loud to yourself as you are going through the rhythm of your day—getting ready, pouring your coffee, waiting in traffic, or making dinner.

Listen to the passage read aloud to you.

Record a voice memo on your phone and listen to it throughout the day or play it on an audio Bible.

SHARE IT

Memorize the passage with a friend, family member, or mentor. Spontaneously challenge each other to recite the passage, or pick a time to review your passage and practice saying it from memory together.

Send the passage as an encouraging text to a friend, testing yourself as you type to see how much you have memorized so far.

KEEP AT IT!

Set reminders on your phone to prompt you to practice your passage.

Purchase a She Reads Truth 12 Card Set or keep a stack of note cards with Scripture you are memorizing by your bed. Practice reciting what you've memorized previously before you go to sleep, ending with the passages you are currently learning. If you wake up in the middle of the night, review them again instead of grabbing your phone. Read them out loud before you get out of bed in the morning.

CSB BOOK ABBREVIATIONS

OLD TESTAMENT

GN Genesis	**JB** Job	**HAB** Habakkuk	**PHP** Philippians
EX Exodus	**PS** Psalms	**ZPH** Zephaniah	**COL** Colossians
LV Leviticus	**PR** Proverbs	**HG** Haggai	**1TH** 1 Thessalonians
NM Numbers	**EC** Ecclesiastes	**ZCH** Zechariah	**2TH** 2 Thessalonians
DT Deuteronomy	**SG** Song of Solomon	**MAL** Malachi	**1TM** 1 Timothy
JOS Joshua	**IS** Isaiah		**2TM** 2 Timothy
JDG Judges	**JR** Jeremiah	**NEW TESTAMENT**	**TI** Titus
RU Ruth	**LM** Lamentations	**MT** Matthew	**PHM** Philemon
1SM 1 Samuel	**EZK** Ezekiel	**MK** Mark	**HEB** Hebrews
2SM 2 Samuel	**DN** Daniel	**LK** Luke	**JMS** James
1KG 1 Kings	**HS** Hosea	**JN** John	**1PT** 1 Peter
2KG 2 Kings	**JL** Joel	**AC** Acts	**2PT** 2 Peter
1CH 1 Chronicles	**AM** Amos	**RM** Romans	**1JN** 1 John
2CH 2 Chronicles	**OB** Obadiah	**1CO** 1 Corinthians	**2JN** 2 John
EZR Ezra	**JNH** Jonah	**2CO** 2 Corinthians	**3JN** 3 John
NEH Nehemiah	**MC** Micah	**GL** Galatians	**JD** Jude
EST Esther	**NAH** Nahum	**EPH** Ephesians	**RV** Revelation

BIBLIOGRAPHY

Barry, John D., David Bomar, Derek R. Brown, Rachel Klippenstein, Douglas Mangum, Carrie Sinclair Wolcott, Lazarus Wentz, Elliot Ritzema, and Wendy Widder, eds. *The Lexham Bible Dictionary.* Bellingham: Lexham Press, 2016.

Brand, Chad, Charles Draper, Archie England, Steve Bond, E. Ray Clendenen, Trent C. Butler, and Bill Latta, eds. *Holman Illustrated Bible Dictionary.* Nashville: Holman Bible Publishers, 2003.

Cox, Steven L., and Kendall H. Easley. *Harmony of the Gospels.* Nashville: Holman Bible Publishers, 2007.

Elwell, Walter A., and Barry J. Beitzel. *Baker Encyclopedia of the Bible.* Grand Rapids: Baker Book House, 1988.

Freedman, David Noel, Gary A. Herion, David F. Graf, John David Pleins, and Astrid B. Beck, eds. *The Anchor Yale Bible Dictionary.* New York: Doubleday, 1992.

Strauss, Mark L. *Four Portraits, One Jesus: An Introduction to Jesus and the Gospels.* Grand Rapids: Zondervan, 2007.

LOOKING FOR DEVOTIONALS?

Download the **She Reads Truth app** to find devotionals that complement your daily Scripture reading. If you're stuck on a passage, hop into the community discussion to connect with other Shes who are reading God's Word right along with you.

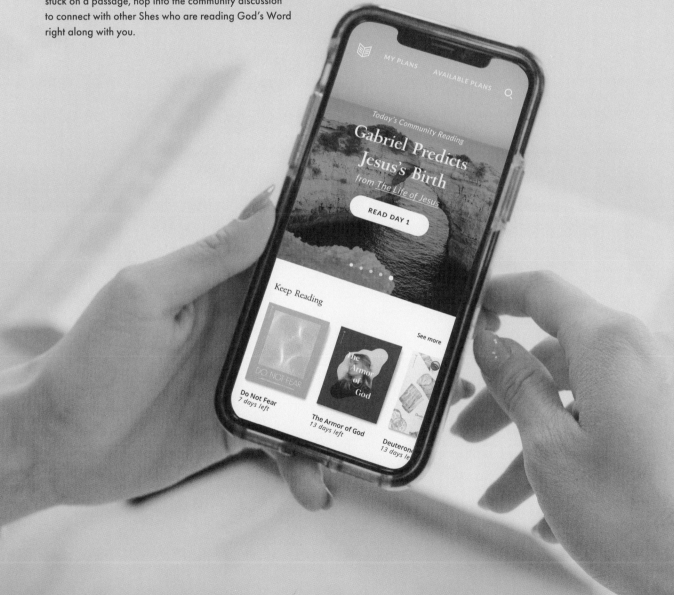

You just spent 35 days in the Word of God!

MY FAVORITE DAY OF
THIS READING PLAN:

ONE THING I LEARNED
ABOUT GOD:

WHAT WAS GOD DOING IN
MY LIFE DURING THIS STUDY?

HOW DID I FIND DELIGHT IN GOD'S WORD?

WHAT DID I LEARN THAT I WANT TO SHARE
WITH SOMEONE ELSE?

A SPECIFIC SCRIPTURE THAT
ENCOURAGED ME:

A SPECIFIC SCRIPTURE THAT
CHALLENGED AND CONVICTED ME: